T0201118

PC Hardware Essentials

Project Manual

RUSSELL POLO

PROJECT EDITOR	Brian B. Baker
MARKETING MANAGER	Jennifer Slomack
PRODUCTION MANAGER	Kelly Tavares
PRODUCTION EDITOR	Kerry Weinstein

Photo Credits: Figures 1-6,1-7, 1-8, 1-9, 1-10, 1-11, 1-12, 1-13, 1-14, 2-2, 5-1, 7-1, 7-4, 7-5, 7-6, 7-7, 7-8, 8-1, 8-2, 8-6, 11-1, 11-2, 11-5, 11-6, 11-9 © Azimuth Interactive, Inc. 2007.

Copyright © 2008 John Wiley & Sons, Inc. All rights reserved. No part of this publication may be reproduced, stored in a retrieval system or transmitted in any form or by any means, electronic, mechanical, photocopying, recording, scanning or otherwise, except as permitted under Sections 107 or 108 of the 1976 United States Copyright Act, without either the prior written permission of the Publisher, or authorization through payment of the appropriate per-copy fee to the Copyright Clearance Center, Inc. 222 Rosewood Drive, Danvers, MA 01923, website www.copyright.com. Requests to the Publisher for permission should be addressed to the Permissions Department, John Wiley & Sons, Inc., 111 River Street, Hoboken, NJ 07030-5774, (201) 748-6011, fax (201) 748-6008, Web site http://www.wiley.com/go/permissions.

To order books or for customer service please call 1-800-CALL WILEY (225-5945).

ISBN 978-0-470-11411-7

Printed in the United States of America

10 9 8 7 6 5 4 3 2 1

Important Note about Completing the Activities in this Manual
For all activities that require documents and other content not included in this printed project manual, please visit the book companion site indicated on the back of this manual. At the website, click on Student Companion Site in the upper right of the webpage, then Project Manual, and then the chapter in which the activity appears.

PREFACE

PC Hardware Essentials Project Manual is a learning tool for individuals who are new to computer hardware, as well as those who seek to expand their skills in the field. It is an ideal companion to Groth et al.'s *PC Hardware Essentials* (Copyright 2008, John Wiley & Sons, 978-0-470-07400-8).

Easy-to-read, practical, and up-to-date, this project manual includes activities that reinforce the fundamentals of computer hardware while helping students develop core competencies and real-world skills. The variety and span of activities allow students to learn at their own pace.

Each chapter contains five to seven projects. Projects range from easy to more advanced, and many include multiple parts. Each project contains the following elements:

- **Overview:** Introduces the topic of the project, and reviews relevant concepts.
- **Outcomes:** Lists what students will know how to do after completing the project.
- **What you'll need:** Lists specific requirements for the project.
- **Completion time:** Provides an estimated completion time as a guide. (Actual completion times may vary depending on experience levels.)
- **Precautions:** Notes on issues that should be taken into account prior to undertaking the project.
- **Projects:** A variety of project types are included. The majority of projects involve hands-on activities in which students are guided through the steps required to accomplish a task. Some projects involve case-based scenarios, while others assess student familiarity with basic concepts through matching and other paper-and-pen exercises. Many of the projects include multiple parts related to the project topic.
- **Assessment questions:** Embedded within each project, these questions help students assess their understanding as they go.
- **Graphic Elements:** Each project contains screenshots, conceptual graphics, and/or tables that help inform and guide students as they proceed through the project.

After completing the activities in this Project Manual, students will be able to:
- use System Properties to determine basic PC configuration
- use Device Manager to determine PC components
- identify basic input and output devices and their connections to a PC
- locate and identify the main internal PC components
- remove and replace drives, drive cables, and expansion cards in a PC
- convert binary and hexidemical numbers to decimal and vice versa
- convert hexadecimal numbers to binary and vice versa
- calculate voltages, currents, and resistances
- use a multimeter to measure DC voltages and perform a continuity check

- remove and install a power supply from a computer
- locate the various components of a motherboard, and identify its type and form factor
- remove and install motherboard
- determine the BIOS version currently installed on a computer
- determine and analyze CPU specifications
- remove and install a CPU
- install a heatsink
- identify a memory module
- examine a system's memory on a Windows 2000 or Windows XP computer
- install a memory module
- identify components of external bus architecture
- use the Device Manager and System Information utility to resolve system resource conflicts
- install both Plug and Play and non-Plug and Play expansion cards
- identify the drive geometry of a hard drive
- use drive geometry information to calculate the available data storage space on the drive
- identify, remove and install an IDE hard drive
- install a SATA hard drive in a computer
- install a SCSI host adapter card, and remove and install a SCSI hard drive
- partition and format a hard disk
- defragment a hard drive
- remove and install a floppy drive from a computer
- install a CD/DVD drive in a computer
- differentiate between different CD and DVD formats, and identify and purchase the appropriate CD/DVD drive
- install, configure and troubleshoot a mouse, keyboard and monitor
- install a video card and sound card
- install and configure a second monitor to your computer system
- install other I/O devices
- install, connect and test a printer
- share a printer
- pause, resume, and cancel printing and send documents to a different printer
- specify the paper sizes for multiple paper trays and set a separator page
- perform preventive maintenance on an inkjet printer and set up a maintenance schedule for a laser printer
- replace a laptop's batteries
- upgrade a laptop's memory
- install a hard disk drive in a laptop
- configure power options on a laptop
- install and remove PC cards in a laptop
- identify the network protocols installed on a computer
- determine the MAC address for a network adapter
- select the most appropriate NIC for a given situation
- install a NIC (wired and wireless)

CONTENTS

1

UNDERSTANDING AND WORKING WITH PERSONAL COMPUTERS

Project 1.1	Finding Basic System Information
Overview	You can determine quite a bit of information about an individual PC through the Windows operating system. When you are troubleshooting a PC, or if you need upgrade a PC by adding or replacing devices, you will need to be able to quickly identify its operating system and determine the types of hardware components it has. There are several simple ways you can gather basic information about a PC: through its startup screens, the System Properties window, and by using the Device Manager. As the computer starts up, you see one or more startup screens display on the monitor before the operating system starts. Depending on the manufacturer, the startup screens may show information about the PC: its system memory, CPU, disk drives, etc. You can temporarily halt the startup process by pressing the Pause key on the keyboard. The Windows System Properties dialog box allows you to review some basic configuration about the computer, such as the operating system that is running and the CPU speed. You can also gain access to an important system utility, the Device Manager, through System Properties. Device Manager lists all the hardware devices, or components, installed in the PC. You can use the Device Manager to check on hardware installed in the computer, to review the status of devices and troubleshoot them, and to configure drivers for devices.
Outcomes	After completing this project, you will know how to: ▲ check the PC's startup screen for system information ▲ use System Properties to determine basic PC configuration ▲ open Device Manager to determine PC components
What you'll need	To complete this project, you will need: ▲ a computer with Windows XP or Windows 2000 installed
Completion time	15 minutes
Precautions	None

■ Part A: Check the startup screen for system information

1. Restart the computer. Open the **Start** menu and select **Shutdown**. On the **Shutdown** screen, select **Restart** to restart the computer.

2. If you see system information displayed in a **Startup** screen (Figure 1-1), press the Pause key and record the information:

Memory/RAM: _____

CPU: _____

Disk Drives: _____

Other: _____

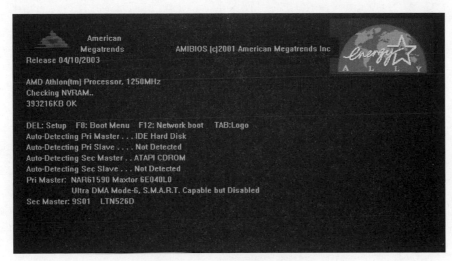

Figure 1-1: PC Startup Screen

3. To continue the startup process, press the Spacebar.

■ Part B: Check basic system information using System Properties

1. To open **System Properties**, right-click **My Computer** on the desktop (or in the **Startup** menu or in **Windows Explorer**) and select **Properties** from the popup menu.

2. Select the **General** tab of the **System Properties** dialog box to display general information about the system. The type of information here varies, depending on the operating system; Window XP displays more information here than earlier operating systems (Figure 1-2).

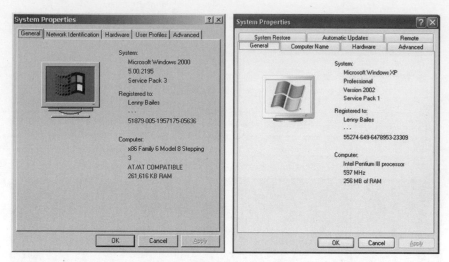

Figure 1-2: Windows 2000 and Windows XP System Properties dialog box

3. Record the information listed on the **General** tab:

    System (Operating system and service pack): _____

    Computer (CPU/RAM): _____

■ Part C: Check hardware devices using Device Manager

1. If it is not open already, open the **System Properties** dialog box by right-clicking **My Computer** on the desktop and selecting **Properties** from the popup menu.
2. Select the **Hardware** tab (Figure 1-3).

Figure 1-3:   Hardware tab of Windows XP System Properties dialog box

3. On the **Hardware** tab, click the Device Manager button to open the **Device Manager** (Figure 1-4).

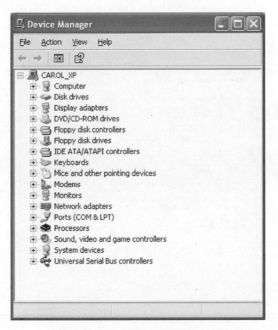

Figure 1-4:   Device Manager

4. In **Device Manager**, make sure that devices are listed according to type. Select **View** on the menu bar and select **Devices by Type** in the dropdown menu.

5. **Device Manager** lists categories of devices as nodes that can be expanded by clicking the + sign beside the category or container. Expand the **Disk Drives** container to see the number of drives listed. For example, there may be several hard disk drives listed under Disk Drives. Explore the categories of devices listed in **Device Manager** and record the devices under the following categories:

   Disk drives: _____

   DVD/CD-ROM drives: _____

   Processors: _____

   Monitors: _____

   Mice and other pointing devices: _____

   Keyboard: _____

6. You can access more information about a particular hardware device through a device's **Properties** dialog box, which you can access through the **Device Manager**. For example, to access the **Properties** dialog box for the PC's monitor, right-click the monitor listed in the **Monitors** node, and select **Properties** from the popup menu. The monitor's **Properties** dialog box will open (Figure 1-5). Review the information here, but do not change any configuration or driver details.

Figure 1-5: Monitor's Properties dialog box

7. Close any **Properties** dialog boxes, **Device Manager**, and then **System Properties**.

Project 1.2	Identifying Input/Output Devices
Overview	When examining and troubleshooting a PC, it is also very important to note what types of external input/output devices are connected to the PC. Common input/output devices for a PC include: • Keyboard • Mouse • Speakers • Microphone • Monitor • Printer • Scanner • Digital camera • External modem
Outcomes	After completing this project, you will know how to: ▲ identify basic input and output devices and their connections to a PC
What you'll need	To complete this project, you will need: ▲ a computer
Completion time	30 minutes
Precautions	During this project, you will need to take careful notes about every device connected to the PC and how it is connected. You will need these notes later to reconnect these devices.

1. Shut down the computer. Open the **Start** menu and select **Shutdown**. On the **Shutdown** screen, select **Turn Off** to turn off the computer.
2. Locate and disconnect the power cable on the back of the PC.
3. List all of the input/output devices attached to the PC in Table 1-1.

Table 1-1: Input/Output Devices

Device	Port Location	Port Details	Type of Port/Connector

4. For each device that you find, trace its cables to the back of the computer system.

5. Use Table 1-1 to record notes on where the device connects to the PC. For example: "Back of PC, top left in row of 5 ports, second from left."

6. For each device:

    a. Disconnect the device from the PC.

    b. Examine the connection at the end of the device cable and the port that it connects to on the PC. In the worktable above or on a separate sheet of paper, record or draw details about the arrangement and number of pins or pinholes, and the shape of the connection or port. For example: "6 pins, round, green port with mouse icon."

    c. Compare the port to the pictures of common ports shown here (Figures 1-6) to identify the type of port the device uses. Record the port type in the work table above.

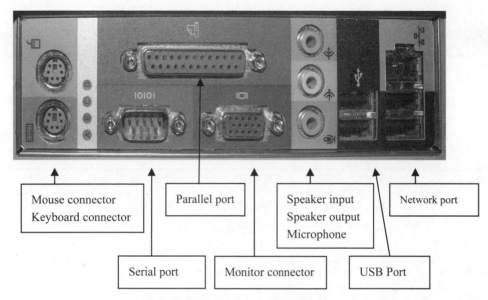

Figure 1-6: Common PC ports

7. After completing this process for each device, use your notes to determine the correct location for reconnecting each device.

8. Carefully connect each device to the computer system. Be careful not to force a connector into a port.

9. After all devices have been reconnected, connect the power cable back to the computer system.

10. Restart the computer system and verify that the devices are working correctly by testing each I/O device. To test the device, perform a simple, common action with each. For example, to test the keyboard, open a text document and type a word. To test a printer, print a sample page.

Project 1.3	Identifying the Internal Components of a PC
Overview	When you are working on a PC, whether you are troubleshooting or upgrading, you will often need to open its case and examine the internal hardware. For example, you may need to check that an internal device is properly attached to the motherboard, or if the motherboard has an appropriate empty slot for a new expansion card. It is important that you are able to quickly identify and locate the internal components of a PC.
Outcomes	After completing this project, you will know how to: ▲ remove and replace the cover of a computer case ▲ protect the computer from static electricity using a wrist strap ▲ locate and identify the main internal PC components
What you'll need	To complete this project, you will need: ▲ a computer (need not be operational) ▲ a technician's toolkit (including Phillips-head screwdriver with medium tip and flashlight) ▲ an antistatic wrist strap and electrostatic discharge (ESD) mat
Completion time	45 minutes
Precautions	To protect the computer from antistatic electricity, it is important to wear an antistatic wrist strap that is connected to the PC case. In addition, before opening the case itself, you should touch the computer with your hand to ground yourself.

1. If the computer is powered on, shut it down. Open the **Start** menu and select **Shutdown**. On the **Shutdown** screen, select **Turn Off** to turn off the computer.

2. Locate and disconnect the power cable on the back of the PC.

3. Determine how the cover of the computer case is removed. Some covers are fastened to the back of the computer by four to six Phillips-head screws. Some cases have latches that you can release and you do not need to unscrew fasteners to open the case. If it is not apparent how the case cover is removed, consult your system manual. If the case cover is attached with screws.

4. Remove any case cover screws using the appropriate screwdriver for the screw type. Place the screws in a secure place. Note the number and location of the system case cover screws.

5. Carefully remove the system case cover. Depending on the type of case you have, you may need to exert some pressure to slide the case off. The computer in Figure 1-7 has a single latch on the back. Slide the latch and one entire side panel of the computer case slides off.

Figure 1-7: Removing a case cover

6. Before touching any components inside the PC, attach the antistatic wrist strap (Figure 1-8) to your wrist. Attach the clip on the end of the wrist strap's cable to a metal part of the PC's case.

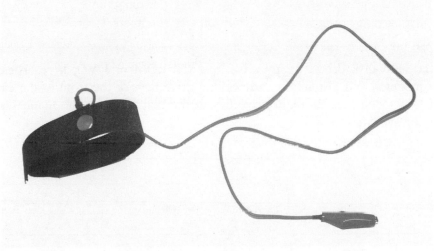

Figure 1-8: Antistatic wrist strap

7.   Locate the power supply (Figure 1-9).

Power supply

Figure 1-9: Power supply inside the PC

8.   The power supply will have several sets of cables. Follow the cables from the power supply to their connections on the motherboard and other devices. One set should be connected to the motherboard, and others may connect to a hard drive, CD-ROM or DVD drive, floppy drive, or a fan mounted on the CPU. Record the number of power cables and the device they connect to, if any.

_____

_____

_____

_____

_____

9.   Locate the hard disk drive, floppy drive, and CD-ROM or DVD drive. These drives are typically mounted and fastened by screws into drive bays at the front of the case, although sometimes there may be an extra drive bay at the rear. Identify the number and types of drives on the system.

_____

_____

_____

_____

_____

_____

10. On the motherboard, locate the CPU, which will usually have a cooling fan or heat sink attached to it. The CPU may be inserted into socket directly on the motherboard or mounted on a card that is inserted into a slot on the motherboard. If there is more than one processor chip that has a heat sink or fan, the largest one is most likely to be the CPU.

11. On the motherboard, locate the RAM memory module slots. Memory module slots are typically in a bank of three or more, long and closely spaced slots with narrow memory boards inserted in them. (You will learn more about different types of RAM memory in Chapter 5.) The RAM slots are typically located somewhere between the CPU and the expansion slots. Record the number of RAM slots you see.

_____

12. On the motherobard, locate the expansion slots. Expansion slots hold larger circuit boards, and there may be several types of expansion slots on the motherboard (Figure 1-10). An older type of expansion slot, the ISA slot, is longer and usually black. PCI slots are a common expansion slot that are usually cream-colored, and newer PCI Express slots may be of varying lengths, some of them quite short compared to PCI slots. Record the number of expansion slots and describe any different types of expansion slots you see.

Figure 1-10: Expansion slots

_____

_____

_____

_____

13. Identify any expansion cards installed in the expansion slots. Common expansion cards are:
    - **Video card:** This will have a port on the back that connects to the monitor
    - **Sound card:** This will have several mini-jack ports for connecting to speakers, microphones, and other audio equipment, with labels for Line In, Line Out, etc.
    - **Internal modem card:** This will have two telephone line (RJ-11) ports to attach a telephone line and telephone receiver.
    - **Network card:** This will have a port similar to a telephone line port, but wider: an RJ-45 port used to attach a network cable.

    Record the types of any expansion cards you find.

    _____

    _____

    _____

    _____

14. On the motherboard, locate the CMOS battery. The CMOS battery is used to store basic PC configuration data when the PC is powered off and usually looks like a large, circular watch battery (Figure 1-11).

Figure 1-11: CMOS battery

15. When you are finished examining the internal components of the PC, unclip the wrist strap from the PC case. Replace the case cover, taking care to reinsert and tighten any case screws. Plug the power cord into the computer.

16. Power the computer on and confirm that it starts up properly.

Project 1.4	Assembling and Reassembling PC Components
Overview	Although PC's themselves are incredibly complex, logical and precisely engineered machines, they are built using many replaceable and upgradeable components that are designed to work together. Given that you have all the necessary and appropriate components—PC case, motherboard, CPU, power supply, hard drives, etc. —working PC's can be relatively easily assembled from scratch. As a PC technician, you will need a firm understanding of how PCs are assembled from these various components, and also how to remove and replace malfunctioning components.
Outcomes	After completing this project, you will know how to: ▲ Remove and replace drives, drive cables, and expansion cards in a PC
What you'll need	To complete this project, you will need: ▲ a Windows computer ▲ a technician's toolkit ▲ an antistatic wriststrap, ESD mat, and clean anti-static workspace suitable for placing internal PC components that are removed from the PC
Completion time	2 hours
Precautions	During this project, take careful notes of all items removed from the system. These notes should be detailed. The position of a striped cable or a screw might make the difference between a functioning and nonfunctioning PC at the end of this project. You will need to use an antistatic wrist strap to protect against static discharge. Make sure you have an adequate workspace, with safe, static-free places to place components while they are removed from the PC. The activities include removing a floppy drive, hard drive, and CD-ROM/DVD drive, in that order. However, depending on the construction of your PC, you may need to remove and replace drives in a different order. If so, make sure to note the order in which you are removing drives, so that you can follow the reverse order when you replace them.

1. If the computer is running, shut the computer down.

2. Remove the power cable from the back of the PC.

3. Disconnect each input/output device from its port. For each device, record the types or locations of the ports these devices connect to on the PC.

   Input/Output Device   Port/Location

   _____ : _____

   _____ : _____

   _____ : _____

   _____ : _____

   _____ : _____

   _____ : _____

   _____ : _____

4. Remove the case cover. If the case cover is attached with screws, note the number and location of screws below and place them in a safe place.

   _____

   _____

   _____

   _____

5. Attach the antistatic wrist band to your wrist and attach its clip to a metal portion of the PC's case.

6. Examine the power supply for any cables that are not attached to a component. For each of these, take notes so that you can remember later, when you are reattaching power cables, which cables should not be attached to anything.

   _____

   _____

   _____

   _____

7. Remove the floppy drive.

   a. Locate the floppy disk drive (FDD). It is usually about 4" by 6" is located at the front of the computer case, with an access slot for inserting floppies. In the FDD workspace below, note the location of the floppy drive.

b. Locate the FDD data cable, typically a wide, flat gray cable with a red stripe along one edge that is attached to the motherboard. This red stripe indicates pin 1 on the data cable and is positioned with the red strip towards the power cable connection on the FDD. It is essential that after the data cable is removed, it is placed back with pin 1 (the red stripe) in the exact same position (Figure 1-12). Note or draw a sketch that indicates the position of the red pin stripe:

Figure 1-12: Floppy drive cable and connector

c. Carefully disconnect the FDD data cable only from the back of the floppy drive.

d. Locate the FDD power cable, which connects to the power supply. Carefully disconnect the FDD power cable only from the back of the floppy drive. Note any keys that are on the cable connector. Keys are identifiable protrusions and matching indentations between the cable connector and its connection on a device that indicate how the cable connector is inserted (Figure 1-13).

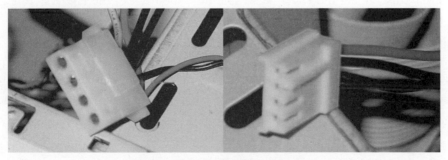

Figure 1-13: Power connectors

e. Examine the FDD to determine how it is attached to the PC. Common mounting methods or mechanisms include screws, drive trays, removable drive bays, and spring-loaded catches. Note the method used for mounting the drive and whether the mounting mechanism is shared with other drives. For example, a floppy drive and hard drive may use a shared removable drive bay.

f. Remove any mounting screws. Note the number and location of screws, any differences between these screws and other screws removed from the PC.

FDD drive location: _____

FDD Pin 1 location: _____

Data cable description and location: _____

Power cable connector description and location: _____

FDD mounting mechanism: _____

Number of FDD mounting screws: _____

Location of FDD mounting screws: _____

Description of FDD mounting screws/differences: _____

g. Carefully remove the FDD from the computer system and place it on a clean, static-free surface. Place any FDD mounting screws beside the FDD so you can identify and locate these screws later.

8. Remove the hard drive.

a. Locate the hard disk drive (HDD). The HDD is usually the same size as the FDD but does not have any access slots.

b. Note the cables connected to the HDD. The data cable for the HDD is connected to the motherboard, and is usually similar to an FDD data cable, with a thin, red stripe indicating pin 1 and facing the same direction—toward the HDD power connector. Note or draw a sketch that indicates the position of the red pin stripe.

c. Carefully disconnect the HDD data cable from the back of the HDD, noting any keys on the connector.

d. Carefully disconnect the HDD power cable, noting any keys on the connector.

e. Examine and record the mounting mechanism used for the HDD. Remove the mounting mechanism, and, if it uses screws, note the number and location of the mounting screws.

f. Carefully remove the HDD and place the HDD on a clean, static free surface, keeping any mounting screws nearby the HDD.

HDD drive location: _____

HDD Pin 1 location: _____

Data cable description and location: _____

Power cable connector description and location: _____

HDD mounting mechanism: _____

Number of HDD mounting screws: _____

Location of HDD mounting screws: _____

Description of HDD mounting screws/differences: _____

9. Remove other drives. Follow the same procedure as the previous step for removing a hard drive. Make sure to note the drive type and where it is located as well as its mounting mechanism, and any screws. Identify its data and power cables, removing each cable from the drive only one at a time, examining the type of connector it uses and any keys that indicate how it is inserted into the drive. Many optical drives also have a third cable used for audio data that may be plugged into an expansion card. Note the location of this cable before removing it from the back of the optical drive.

Drive type (CD, DVD, etc): _____

Drive location: _____

Data cable Pin 1 location (if any): _____

Data cable description and location: _____

Power cable connector description and location: _____

Drive mounting mechanism: _____

Number of mounting screws: _____

Location of mounting screws: _____

Description of mounting screws/differences: _____

Additional cables and placement notes: _____

10. Remove the data cables from the motherboard. For each drive that you removed:

a. Follow its data cable to the motherboard and note the location of the connection on the motherboard, including the relative position of the red striped edge of the cable. Keep notes or draw a sketch so that you can be sure to replace each data cable in its correct location on the motherboard:

b. Carefully remove each data cable from the motherboard. Some may have a catch that you need to release first (by pressing the edges of the connector, for example).

FDD motherboard data connector location: _____

HDD motherboard data connector location: _____

CD/DVD motherboard data connector location: _____

Other motherboard data connector location: _____

11. Examine and remove the expansion cards on the motherboard. Draw a sketch showing the location of the installed expansion cards. For each of the expansion cards, starting with the card that is furthest from the CPU, perform the following steps:

a. Note the expansion card's type (video, sound, etc.), and describe or sketch the location and general appearance (relative length, color, etc.) of its slot, so that you can remember where to reinsert them later.

b. Remove any screws that attach the expansion card to the back of the PC case (Figure 1-14). In the expansion card workspace below, record and describe the number and types of screws, so that you can identify these when replacing the card.

Figure 1-14: Screw attaching expansion card to case

c. If any cables are connected to an expansion card, note the location of the connector on the card, and carefully remove this cable. Be sure to note the description of the cable and its location in your notes on the expansion card, so that you can replace this cable later.

d. Remove the expansion card from its slot. Be careful not to rock or twist the card as you remove it, as this could damage the slot. Place the card on a clean, static-free surface.

Expansion card location sketch:

_____

Expansion card 1

Type: _____

Location of slot on motherboard: _____

Description of slot: _____

Attached cables: _____

Number of screws for case attachment: _____

Description of screws: _____

Expansion card 2

Type: _____

Location of slot on motherboard: _____

Description of slot: _____

Attached cables: _____

Number of screws for case attachment: _____

Description of screws: _____

Expansion card 3

Type: _____

Location of slot on motherboard: _____

Description of slot: _____

Attached cables: _____

Number of screws for case attachment: _____

Description of screws: _____

Expansion card 4

Type: _____

Location of slot on motherboard:_____

Description of slot: _____

Attached cables: _____

Number of screws for case attachment: _____

Description of screws: _____

12. With the hard drives and expansion cards out of the system, examine the motherboard and any additional cables running from the motherboard to the power supply or to the front or back panel of the computer, for example, to a USB port in the front of the case. List and describe the types of cables you see and whether they are attached to anything.

_____

_____

_____

_____

_____

13 Reinstall the expansion cards. For each expansion card:

    a.   Carefully reinsert the card into the slot it was taken from.

    b.   Reattach any cables that were removed from the expansion slot.

    c.   Reattach the expansion card to the PC case using any screws removed.

14. Review your reinstallation of expansion cards: Using your notes, confirm that:

    a.   The expansion card locations and placement match your sketch.

    b.   All screws and cables have been reattached to their original positions.

15. Reattach the drive data cables to the motherboard. For each data cable:

    a.   Identify the drive connector on the motherboard. For any FDD or HDD ribbon cables, locate pin 1 on each motherboard connector.

    b.   Reinsert the data cable into its motherboard connector. Make sure that any data ribbon cables with a red stripe are positioned so that the red stripe is toward pin 1.

16. Reinstall drives. For each drive:

    a.   Use your notes to locate the drive's original placement and mounting mechanism.

    b.   Insert the drive into its original position.

    c.   Carefully reinsert the drive's power cable into the drive, making sure that the key on the cable connector is aligned with the key on the drive's connector.

    d.   Carefully reinsert the data cable into the drive, making sure to position ribbon cables with red stripes in the same position as before—with the red stripe closest to the power connector on the drive.

    e.   Reattach any audio cables to a CD or DVD drive.

    f.   Reattach the mounting mechanism to the PC's case, making sure to use all screws removed previously.

17. Review your installation of the hard drives. Make sure that each drive has at least two cables attached, one to the motherboard and the other to the power supply. If there are unattached cables running from the motherboard or power supply, account for them by using your previous notes on these cables. Check that there are no leftover components, cables, or screws (except for any PC case screws and external cables to input/output devices) on your worktable or workspace.

18. Reattach any input/output device cables to the back of the computer.

19. Disconnect the clip on the antistatic wrist strap from the computer and the strap from your writs.

20. Reattach the power cable to the computer.

21. With the cover of the case still off, power up the PC and confirm that all devices are working. Make sure that the keyboard, mouse, monitor, and speakers work and that you can access any drives and insert any CDs or DVDs and read these.

22. If any device is not working, the most likely cause is a loose connection of its data or power cable. Power down the computer, reattach the antistatic wrist strap. Use your notes to review the installation of cables and devices and check that its cable connections are firmly seated into the proper connection.

23. When you have confirmed that the computer system is working properly, replace the cover, making sure that you use all of the original screws.

Project 1.5	Working with Binary Numbers
Overview	In computing, electrical charges, or on and off states, are used to represent 1s and 0s and are manipulated using the binary number system. Binary numbers are used because it is far easier for computer components to be engineered to produce and detect the difference between the strengths of two electrical charges rather detect the difference between ten signals representing a decimal number system. Understanding the binary number system is essential to understanding how computers work and how they transfer and process data as bits (1s or 0s) and bytes (groups of bits, typically 8). Binary values are the result of the number 2 being raised to various powers. This is true for all number systems. The decimal number system is based on values of the number 10 raised to increasing powers. For example, 2^2 is 8, and 2^{10} is 1024.
Outcomes	After completing this project, you will know how to: ▲ convert binary numbers to decimal ▲ convert decimal numbers to binary
What you'll need	To complete this project, you will need: ▲ the worksheet below
Completion time	30 minutes
Precautions	None

■ Part A: Converting Binary to Decimal

In converting a binary number such as 00000101 to a decimal value , the key is to remember that each position represents a successive power of 2, starting with 2^0 on the furthest right, and continuing with 2^1, 2^2, 2^3 and up. For example, the binary number 1010 contains

$0 * 2^0 = 0$ (any number to the zero power is worth 1)

$1 * 2^1 = 2$ (any number to the one power is the number)

$0 * 2^2 = 0$ (two times two)

$1 * 2^3 = 8$ (two times two times two)

Totaling 10 (the remaining positions are all zero)

Another way to express this relationship, for the binary number 1010, is shown in Table 1-2:

Table 1-2: Converting Binary to Decimal

Binary Number	1	0	1	0
Bit Position	4	3	2	1
Power	3	2	1	0
Weight	2^3	2^2	2^1	2^0
Decimal Value	8		2	

Use Table 1-3 to compute the decimal values for the following binary numbers.

1. 101101   Decimal equivalent: _____

2. 11011001   Decimal equivalent: _____

3. 10010010011   Decimal equivalent: _____

Table 1-3: Decimal Values for Various Powers of Two

Position	Power	Decimal Value
0	2^0	1
1	2^1	2
2	2^2	4
3	2^3	8
4	2^4	16
5	2^5	32
6	2^6	64
7	2^7	128
8	2^8	256
9	2^9	512
10	2^{10}	1024

■ Part B: Converting Decimal to Binary

One way to convert a decimal number to a binary number is to divide the decimal number by two repeatedly. After each division step, you place either a 1 or a 0, starting from the far right (bit position 0). You place a 1, if there is a remainder of 1 (the number is indivisible by 2) and 0 if there is a remainder of 0 (the number is divisible by 2). The division process is continued until the final number to be divided is 0.

For example, to convert 279 into decimal:

1. Divide the original number, 279, by 2: 279/2 = 139, remainder 1. The remainder 1 is placed at the first bit position: 1

2. Divide the results of the previous step by 2: 139/2 = 69, remainder 1. Again, the remainder 1 is placed at the next bit position: 11

3. 69/2 = 34, remainder 1. A 1 is placed at the next bit position: 111

4. 34/2 = 17, remainder 0. A 0 is placed at the next bit position: 0111

5. 17/2 = 8, remainder 1:   10111

6. 8/2 = 4, remainder 0:   010111

7. 4/2 = 2, remainder 0:   0010111

8. 2/2 = 1, remainder 0.   00010111

9. 1/2 = 0, remainder 1.   100010111

10. 0/2: Because the final number reached is 0, the division process is ended. The binary equivalent of 279 is 100010111.

Convert the following decimal numbers into binary:

1. 37   Binary equivalent: _____

2. 149   Binary equivalent: _____

3. 614   Binary equivalent: _____

Project 1.6	Working with Hexadecimal Numbers
Overview	Computer programmers often work with the hexadecimal number system, which uses 16 as its base number (instead of 10 as in decimal or 2 as in binary). The hexadecimal number system is used because bits are often stored and processed in groups of 16: Using 16 as a base number allows for more compact manipulation and storage of data. The hexadecimal system uses 6 additional characters: A= 10 B = 11 C= 12 D=13 E=14 F=15 Hexadecimal numbers are often designated by a small h following the number, as in 5AEh, to distinguish them from decimal numbers.
Outcomes	After completing this project, you will know how to: ▲ convert hexadecimal numbers to decimal ▲ convert decimal numbers to hexadecimal ▲ convert hexadecimal numbers to binary ▲ convert binary numbers to hexadecimal
What you'll need	To complete this project, you will need: ▲ the worksheet below
Completion time	30 minutes

■ Part A: Converting Hexadecimal to Decimal

To convert a hexadecimal number to decimal, add the values of the hexadecimal number at each position in the number. To determine the values of the hexadecimal number at each position, multiply the value of the hexadecimal number (which may be 0 through F, or in decimal, 0 through 15) by its position value. Each position value represents a power of 16 (Table 1-4).

For example, hexadecimal number A5Bh contains:

$B \times 16^0 = B \times 1 = 11 \times 1 = 11$

$5 \times 16^1 = 5 \times 16 = 80$

$A \times 16^2 = A \times 256 = 10 \times 256 = 2560$

For a total decimal equivalent of: 2651

Table 1-4: Decimal Values for Various Powers of 16

Position	Power	Decimal Value
0	16^0	1
1	16^1	16
2	16^2	256
3	16^3	4096
4	16^4	65536

Convert the following hexadecimal numbers to decimal, referring to Table 1-4 to determine the decimal values for each position of the hexadecimal number.

1. FA7h   Decimal equivalent: _____

2. B2h   Decimal equivalent: _____

3. 92Dh   Decimal equivalent: _____

■ Part B: Converting Decimal to Hexadecimal

To convert a decimal number to hexadecimal, you can follow the same principle as converting decimal to binary, of dividing the number repeatedly by the base number 16. The remainders after each division are placed as values in successive positions.

For example, to convert 2909 into hexadecimal:

1. Divide 279 by 16: 279/16 = 181, remainder 13, or, in hexadecimal, D. The remainder D is placed at the first position: D

2. Divide the results of the previous step by 16: 181/16 = 11, remainder 5. The remainder 5 is placed at the next position: 5D

3. 11/16 = 0, remainder 11, or B. A B is placed at the next position: B5D

4. 0/16: Because the final number reached is 0, the division process is ended. The hexadecimal equivalent of 2909 is B5D.

Convert the following decimal numbers into hexadecimal:

1. 64   Hexadecimal equivalent: _____

2. 5012   Hexadecimal equivalent: _____

3. 1045   Hexadecimal equivalent: _____

■ Part C: Converting Hexadecimal to Binary

The process for converting hexadecimal to binary is very simple. Each hexadecimal position translates to four binary positions (Table 1-5). To convert a hexadecimal to binary, you convert each hexadecimal position to its binary equivalent, and then join the value strings for the binary equivalents together. For example, to convert the hexadecimal number, 5B, you join the binary equivalents for 5 (0101) and B (1011) together in the same order: 01011011, or, omitting the first 0s, 1011011.

Table 1-5: Hexadecimal and Binary Equivalents

HEX	BINARY
0	0000
1	0001
2	0010
3	0011
4	0100
5	0101
6	0110
7	0111
8	1000
9	1001
A	1010
B	1011
C	1100
D	1101
E	1110
F	1111

Use this process and Table 1-5 to convert the following hexadecimal numbers to binary:

1. 6AE   Binary equivalent: _____

2. 7D   Binary equivalent: _____

3. 9F33   Binary equivalent: _____

■ Part D: Converting Binary Numbers to Hexadecimal

To convert binary to hexadecimal, you reverse the process used in converting hexadecimal to binary. First, group the binary numbers into groups of 4, adding trailing 00s at the left positions in order to maintain 4 digits in each group. You must make sure to start from the rightmost digit to create these groups.

Example: To convert 110111 to hexadecimal:

1. Separate the binary digits into groups of four: 0011 and 0111.
2. Replace each group with its hexadecimal value. 0011 is 3h and 0111 is 7h, which makes a hexadecimal equivalent of 37h.

   Use this process and Table 1-5 to convert the following binary numbers to hexadecimal:

   a. 1100101   Hexadecimal equivalent: _____

   b. 110010110   Hexadecimal equivalent: _____

   c. 1110110010   Hexadecimal equivalent: _____

2

ELECTRICITY AND POWER

Project 2.1	Calculating Electrical Measurements
Overview	In this project, you will learn to work with some common electrical measurements as they apply to computers. The units you will be working with are: • Amps: measure a current's strength or rate of flow • Ohms: measure a conductor's resistance to electricity • Volts: measure the electrical pressure in a circuit • Watts: measure the electrical power in a circuit range The formulas that you will need to know are: • Volts = Amps * Ohms • Watts = Volts * Amps
Outcomes	After completing this project, you will know how to: ▲ calculate voltages, currents, and resistances
What you'll need	To complete this project, you will need: ▲ the worksheet below
Completion time	30 minutes
Precautions	None

1. First, to derive formulas in terms of Amps and Ohms, use the following formula for calculating volts

   Volts = Amps * Ohms.

   _____

2. If a circuit has a resistance of 10 ohms and produces a 4.0 amp current, what is its voltage?

   _____

3. If a circuit is generating 128 volts and has a resistance of 16 ohms, what is its current?

   _____

4. If a circuit is generating 85 volts and produces a 5.0 amp current, what is its resistance?

   _____

5. Now, calculate the power (wattage) of the circuits in questions 2, 3, and 4, using the formula Watts = Volts * Amps.

   _____

6. If a circuit produces 432 watts and produces a 4.0 amp current, what is its resistance?

_____

7. Which has more power: a spark of static electricity on the order of 400,000 volts with 0.001 amps of current, or a welder using 110 volts and 75 amps?

_____

Project 2.2	Using a Multimeter
Overview	A multimeter is an invaluable tool when it comes to ensuring that the correct voltages are being passed to a device or computer. It helps you determine whether the problems you may be experiencing are the result of faulty power or a faulty device. If the proper voltages are not being delivered, the devices cannot function properly. You can also use a multimeter to perform continuity checks on cables. A continuity check gives you a quick indication of whether a wire is broken. If you get a reading of 0 ohms, the wire is good. If the reading is infinite, there is a break in the cable. The same check can be performed on a fuse to see if it is still good.
Outcomes	After completing this project, you will know how to: ▲ use a multimeter to measure DC voltages ▲ use a multimeter to perform a continuity check
What you'll need	To complete this project, you will need: ▲ a working computer ▲ a technician's toolkit ▲ an IDE cable ▲ an antistatic wrist strap and ESD mat
Completion time	60 minutes
Precautions	When measuring voltage, be sure you connect the probes to the power source correctly. With DC voltage, the red probe must connect to the positive side and the black probe to the negative. You must also make sure to change the selector to VDC (Volts DC) or VAC (Volts AC), as these settings protect the meter from overload. Do not plug a meter into a power supply while it's still set to measure resistance. Doing so may blow the meter.

> Be sure to set the multimeter to read voltage before attempting to measure voltage; if it is set to read current when you attempt to read voltage, you will seriously damage the multimeter.
>
> Do not test resistance on components when they are mounted on a circuit board. The multimeter applies a current to the component being tested, which may flow to other components on the board, and damage then.
>
> Also, make sure to use your antistatic wrist strap and connect it to a static ground mat or the PC case.

1. Prepare the multimeter (Figure 2-1) for use. If the multimeter has detachable leads, connect the black lead to the negative jack and the red lead to the positive jack on the multimeter. Follow the multimeter directions to accurately set the zero point on the multimeter.

Meter

Function
Selector Switch

Red (+)
Probe

Black (−)
Probe

Figure 2-1: A common multimeter

2. Set the multimeter to measure DC voltages.
3. Set the meter to read for voltages less than 20VDC.
4. Shut down the computer and unplug it.
5. Remove the system cover. Attach your antistatic wrist strap to the computer case.
6. Locate a Molex power connector. It will have two black wires, one red wire, and one yellow wire. The black wires are ground wires. You will determine the voltage carried on the red and yellow wires.

7. Connect the black multimeter lead to one of the black wires and the red multimeter lead to the red wire (Figure 2-2).

Figure 2-2: Using a multimeter to test the voltage carried by a Molex connector

8. Plug in the computer and turn on the power. Observe the voltage reading of the red wire and record it.

_____

9. Shut down the computer and unplug it.
10. Leave the black multimeter lead connected to a black wire. Move the red multimeter lead to the yellow wire.
11. Plug in the computer and turn on the power. Observe the voltage reading of the yellow wire and record it.

_____

12. Shut down the computer and unplug it.
13. To measure continuity, if you have an extra IDE cable, you can use it; otherwise remove an IDE cable from your computer. Note the location of pin 1 on both the IDE controller on the motherboard and on the IDE devices.
14. Change the setting on the multimeter to read Ohms.
15. Place one lead on one end of pin 1 and the other lead at the other end of pin 1 (Figure 2-3) and record the reading.

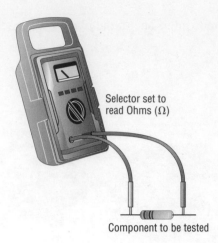

Selector set to
read Ohms (Ω)

Component to be tested

Figure 2-3: Connecting a multimeter to measure ohms

16. If you removed the IDE cable, replace it in the computer. Take care to ensure that pin 1 is connected to pin 1 on the IDE controller on the motherboard and to the pin 1 on the IDE device.

Project 2.3	Determining an Appropriate Power Supply
Overview	When building a computer or replacing a power supply for a current computer, choosing an appropriate power supply can be a difficult task. It is also a very important one. In this project, you will familiarize yourself with the task of determining the power needs of a computer and choosing an appropriate power supply for the computer. Note that in addition to power requirements, motherboard/CPU power connector types also determine the power supply that should be purchased—these considerations are addressed in Project 2.4.
Outcomes	After completing this project, you will know how to: ▲ choose an appropriate power supply for your system and motherboard
What you'll need	To complete this project, you will need: ▲ an antistatic wrist strap ▲ a technician's toolkit
Completion time	60 minutes
Precautions	This project requires you to open the computer cover. As usual, take proper precautions to guard against ESD.

1. Shut down the computer.

2. Turn off the power to all peripherals that are attached to the computer.

3. Sketch the back of the computer as you disconnect all external cables.

_____

4. Remove the computer cover.

5. Attach the anti-static wrist strap to the computer case.

6. Observe the devices inside your computer. Some of the devices should be marked with their power requirements. For some devices, such as the motherboard, this information will not be readily available. If the device is not marked, but you can determine the manufacturer, you can sometimes find this information on the manufacturer's website. Be sure to include the computer's internal fans. Whenever possible, mark down the amounts that each device requires.

_____

_____

_____

7. Add up these amounts to determine how much power your system requires. For the devices that were not marked with their power requirements, make a reasonable estimate, and add them to your total. For example, the motherboard could require anywhere from 100 to 200 watts by itself, depending upon the sophistication of the computer. Show your work.

_____

_____

8. Determine the power supply of your computer. Does it provide adequate power for the system? Use your answer for question 7 to explain why.

_____

_____

9. Assume that you need to build a new computer. The motherboard requires 100 watts. The computer will use a total of 10 other devices, which have power requirements of the following: 50 watts, 40 watts, 35.5 watts, 26.5 watts, 20 watts, 18 watts, 15.5 watts, 13.5 watts, 10 watts, and 8 watts. You have three power supplies to choose from: a 250 watt power supply, a 300 watt power supply, and a 350 watt power supply. Which one would you choose and why? Explain your answer.

_____

_____

_____

_____

Project 2.4	Comparing Power Supplies
Overview	When shopping for power supplies you will find a wide variety of choices. In this project you will learn more about the market place for power supplies, and how to purchase a power supply that meets your specific requirements. Online retailers are generally excellent sources of information, so you will use the Internet to complete this project.
Outcomes	After completing this project, you will know how to: ▲ choose between different power supplies
What you'll need	To complete this project, you will need: ▲ a computer with access to the Internet
Completion time	30 minutes
Precautions	None

1. Go online and search for 'power supply' or 'computer power supply'. Find an online retailer with a large selection of power supplies.

2. Pick three power supplies and obtain the following information about them: total wattage, supported motherboards, number of connectors, supported pin connections to the motherboard (20-pin, 24-pin, or both), and the price. If some of this information is unavailable, keep searching for power supplies until you can gather the required information. Try to find three options with different specifications; if some of your options are very similar to each other, find another power supply with different specifications. Make sure that at least one of the power supplies that you choose can support a multiprocessor system.

Power Supply 1

Name: _____

Total Wattage: _____

Number of Connectors: _____

Supported Pin Connections: _____

Price: _____

Power Supply 2

Name: _____

Total Wattage: _____

Number of Connectors: _____

Supported Pin Connections: _____

Price: _____

Power Supply 3

Name: _____

Total Wattage: _____

Number of Connectors: _____

Supported Pin Connections: _____

Price: _____

3. Assume that you recently purchased a high-end computer, but the power supply unexpectedly failed. You want to acquire a new power supply, but it has to be able to provide as much power as possible to your system. Which of your three choices would you select and why?

_____

_____

_____

_____

_____

4. Assume that you're the administrator of a small network of computers. You are told that the network will need to be able to handle as many peripherals as possible, and as a result you need to acquire new power supplies that have a large number of connectors. Price is no object, since without the necessary connections, the machines won't work properly. Which of your three choices would you select and why?

    _____

    _____

    _____

    _____

    _____

5. Assume that your power supply needs replacing, but you don't want to spend a great deal of money on a new power supply. However, you've calculated that you will need a power supply capable of producing at least 500 watts. Also, it must be compatible with a 20-pin connection to the motherboard. Of your three choices, which one would you select and why?

    _____

    _____

    _____

    _____

Project 2.5	Removing a Power Supply
Overview	Power supplies generally require little to no maintenance, but situations may arise in which it is useful to remove the power supply and replace it with a new one. This is can be a dangerous procedure, so be sure to adhere to the precautions listed below.
Outcomes	After completing this project, you will know how to: ▲ remove a power supply from a computer
What you'll need	To complete this project, you will need: ▲ a computer with a power supply ▲ a technician's toolkit that includes a non-magnetic Phillips-head screwdriver ▲ a container to hold removed screws ▲ an antistatic wrist strap

Completion time	30 minutes
Precautions	AT form factor computers have 120 volts applied to the panel-mounted power switch any time the power cable is attached to the computer. The voltage is a safety hazard to the technician. If you come in contact with the 120 volts, serious injury or death could occur. The AT form factor has become basically obsolete.
	ATX/NLX form factor computers have 5 volts on the motherboard any time the computer is attached to the power cable. The ATX12V is an updated version of the ATX form factor. It adds an extra 4-pin +12 volt power connector, called the P4 connector, which enables the delivery of more current needed by the higher-end processors. The voltage is a safety hazard to the motherboard when the case is open. If a screw or some other object drops into the computer and short-circuits the motherboard, the motherboard will be destroyed.
	Make sure not to plug the power supply into a wall outlet unless it is connected to a motherboard! Doing so could produce high voltage and cause the power supply to self-destruct.
	This project requires the computer cover to be removed. As a result, proper ESD precautions must also be taken to ensure that the sensitive components of the computer are not damaged.

1. Sketch the back of the computer and show where each cable is attached. Then, disconnect all the external cables from the computer, including the power cable.

2. Remove the computer cover to expose the power supply (Figure 2-4). Attach your antistatic wrist strap to the computer case.

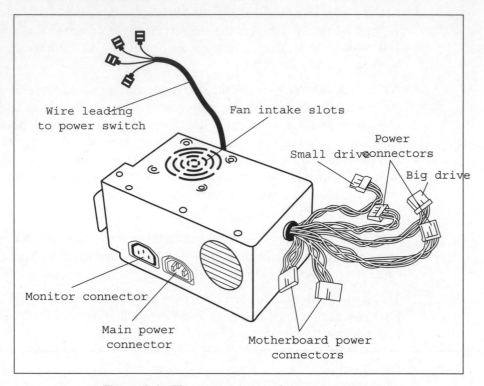

Figure 2-4: The components of a power supply

3. Sketch the power supply's cabling and connections.

---

4. Disconnect the power supply connector(s) from the motherboard. AT/Baby AT form factors have two power connectors (P8 and P9) on the motherboard. If working with an AT/Baby AT form factor, note the relative position of P8 and P9 so they can be reassembled properly later. ATX/NLX computers have one power connector on the motherboard. Early ATXV12 may have an auxiliary connector as well. Newer ATX12V power supplies use a 24-pin connector that combines the old standard 20-pin ATX connector and the auxiliary connector. The newest power supplies may also have a PCI express connector, a 6-pin connector used to power newer PCI express graphics cards or a 15-pin connector for powering newer SATA drives.

5. Disconnect the other power-supply cable leads from the drives, fans, and so on.

6. Each piece of hardware that you disconnect must be reconnected to the replacement power supply. In the space below, make a list of the hardware items as you disconnect them so you can use the list as a guide when you reassemble the computer.

_____

_____

_____

_____

7. The power switch is located on the front panel of most computers. If the power switch cable is directly connected to the power supply, remove the switch from the case and *leave it connected to the power supply*.

    Note: If for some reason you decided to disconnect the power supply cable from the front panel switch, make sure that you diagram how the black, blue, white, and brown wires are connected to the switch. If you reconnect things backwards, you could cause a short circuit that could make your computer catch fire.

8. Begin to remove the four power-supply mounting screws that hold the power supply in place. As you do, make sure that you support the power supply by holding it with your free hand until all the screws have been removed. Then lift the power supply out of the case.

Project 2.6	Installing a Power Supply
Overview	In this project, you will replace the power supply you removed in Project 2.5. Once again, working with power supplies can be dangerous if the proper precautions are not observed.
Outcomes	After completing this project, you will know how to: ▲ install a power supply
What you'll need	To complete this project, you will need: ▲ the power supply and mounting screws that you removed in Project 2.5 ▲ an antistatic wrist strap ▲ a technician's toolkit with anti-magnetic Phillips head screwdriver
Completion time	30 minutes
Precautions	The same precautions that applied in Project 2.5 are still relevant here

1. Wear an antistatic wrist strap to protect the computer from ESD, and make sure no external cables are connected to the computer or the power supply.

2. Place the power supply in the computer case's power-supply support bracket (see Figure 2-5), and then install the mounting screws. You may want to consider dusting the power supply, as dust collection can contribute to the degradation of the power supply. Take the nozzle of a vacuum and remove as much dust as possible from the power supply.

Figure 2-5: Installing a power supply

3. For an ATX/NLX/ATXv12 computer, the power switch connects to the motherboard.

4. For an AT/BabyAT computer, route the power-switch cable in a safe location, and attach the power switch to the case.

5. Attach the power supply to the motherboard.

6. If you have an AT/BabyAT computer, attach connectors P8 and P9 to the motherboard with the black wires next to each other. If the P8 and P9 connectors are reversed, the motherboard will probably be destroyed.

7. On an ATX computer, the motherboard power connector is keyed and will fit only one way.

8. Remove your antistatic wrist strap, replace the computer case, and connect the external cables to the computer.

9. Attempt to boot the computer. Does it boot?

_____

3

MOTHERBOARDS

Project 3.1	Comparing Motherboards
Overview	When something goes wrong with a motherboard, or when it comes time to replace an outdated motherboard, you will need to be able to determine what type of replacement motherboard is most appropriate. In this project, you will use the web to research different types of motherboards and gather information about them.
Outcomes	After completing this project, you will know how to: ▲ compare motherboards in terms of their components
What you'll need	To complete this project, you will need: ▲ a computer with Internet access
Completion time	30 minutes
Precautions	None

1. Open up a web browser and go to an online PC components retailer. Tiger Direct, or NewEgg are a good examples, but any web search for 'motherboards' or 'computer parts' will yield additional choices.

2. Choose three motherboards from the website, and for each one, fill out the information below. If the website does not have all of this information for one of the boards you picked, try a different one, or move to a different website that has this information. For instance, you may want to check the motherboard manufacturer's website. Make sure that at least one of the motherboards you choose supports multiprocessors.

Motherboard 1:

Form factor: _____

Type of CPU supported:_____

CPU speeds supported: _____

Socket format: _____

Memory type/speed/maximum size supported: _____

Number of memory slots: _____

Internal storage support (IDE, SATA, SCSI): _____

Number of total expansion slots: _____

Northbridge chipset: _____

On-board features (video, network, audio): _____

External interfaces/ports: _____

Price: _____

Motherboard 2:

Form factor: _____

Type of CPU supported:_____

CPU speeds supported: _____

Socket format: _____

Memory type/speed/ maximum size supported: _____

Number of memory slots: _____

Internal storage support (IDE, SATA, SCSI): _____

Number of total expansion slots: _____

Northbridge chipset: _____

On-board features (video, network, audio): _____

External interfaces/ports: _____

Price: _____

Motherboard 3:

Form factor: _____

Type of CPU supported:_____

CPU speeds supported: _____

Socket format: _____

Memory type/speed/maximum size supported: _____

Number of memory slots: _____

Internal storage support (IDE, SATA, SCSI): _____

Number of total expansion slots: _____

Northbridge chipset: _____

On-board features (video, network, audio): _____

External interfaces/ports: _____

Price: _____

3. Which of the three motherboards would you pick if you wanted to maximize your system's memory and why?

_____

_____

_____

4. Which of the three motherboards would you pick if you wanted to maximize your system's speed and why?

_____

_____

_____

_____

5. Which of the three motherboards would you pick if you wanted to be able to add as many expansion cards as possible and why?

_____

_____

_____

6. Which of the three motherboards would you pick if you were on a very tight budget and why?

_____

_____

_____

Project 3.2	Examining a Motherboard
Overview	Motherboards may vary in several important ways, but all of them share some key components. All motherboards have a chipset, buses, memory slots, and chips, expansion slots and cards, ports and connectors, and a CPU. The configuration of these items determines a motherboard's type. In this project, you will examine a motherboard, carefully observing its features, and determine what its form factor (see Figure 3-1 for an example of a board with the ATX form factor) and type are. You will also familiarize yourself with the various components of a motherboard.
Outcomes	After completing this project, you will know how to: ▲ locate the various components of a motherboard ▲ identify the type and form factor of a motherboard
What you'll need	To complete this project, you will need: ▲ a working computer ▲ a technician's toolkit ▲ an antistatic wrist strap
Completion time	60 minutes
Precautions	As soon as the computer cover is removed, ESD (electrostatic discharge) becomes a hazard to the computer. For this reason, you should prepare a static-free location to perform this project. Wear an antistatic wrist strap and attach it to the computer case. If no antistatic wrist strap is available, equalize the static charge by frequently touching a bare portion of the computer case. Failure to do this could disable certain components of the motherboard. Additionally, you may want to keep detailed notes throughout this project in case you have trouble replacing the motherboard with its initial configuration. The most difficult part of motherboard removal and replacement is keeping track of what goes where. Do not rely on your memory. Take notes, draw diagrams, and mark wires as you remove components. Without this information, reassembly becomes a guessing game. Confirm that your computer is operational before you open the computer case and after you complete the project.

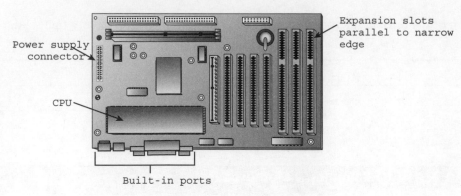

Figure 3-1: Motherboard with ATX form factor

1. Disconnect the power cord from the computer's power supply.

2. Remove the computer case cover.

3. Attach the antistatic wrist strap to a metal portion of the system case.

4. Carefully observe the system board. If necessary, disconnect cables to make locating the necessary items easier. If you disconnect any cables, make sure to record the cable that was removed.

5. Locate the microprocessor and the chipset chips (see Figure 3-2 for a schematic of a Pentium motherboard to help orient yourself, if necessary). Notice the location of the chipset's two chips. Typically, the Northbridge is located somewhere near both the microprocessor and the memory slots and often has a heat sink and cooling fan. The Southbridge is frequently located at one end of the expansion slots.

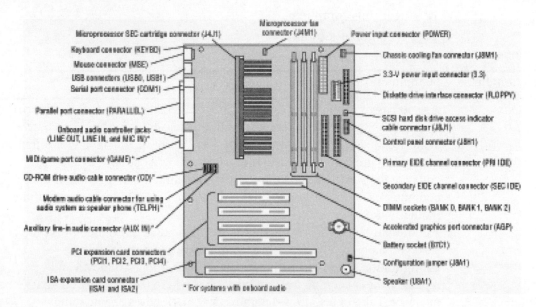

Figure 3-2: The components of a motherboard

6. How many RAM slots can you find?

    _____

7. Locate the expansion slots. Slot types might include:
    *   8- and 16-bit Industry Standard Architecture (ISA) (black slots) (Note that these will primarily be found in older computers.)
    *   Peripheral Component Interconnect (PCI) (white or cream slots)
    *   Accelerated Graphics Port (AGP) (brown slots)
    *   PCI Express slots
8. How many expansion slots can you find? What type are they?

    _____

    _____

9. Locate any other interfaces on the motherboard. Other interfaces might include:
    *   IDE (Integrated Device Electronics)
    *   Floppy disk controller
    *   USB (Universal Serial Bus
    *   FireWire (IEEE Institute of Electrical and Electronics Engineers) 1394
    *   SATA (Serial ATA)
    *   SCSI (Small Computer System Interface)

10. Does your motherboard have these items?

    IDE: _____

    Floppy disk controller: _____

    USB: _____

    FireWire: _____

    SATA: _____

    SCSI: _____

11. Create a schematic diagram containing these items, labeled appropriately, in the space below.

    _____

12. Review the schematic noting the position of the microprocessor as compared to the expansion slots. Using this along with the approximate size of the motherboard, determine which form factor was used in the design of your motherboard and add it as a label onto the schematic diagram.

Project 3.3	Removing a Motherboard
Overview	The motherboard contains or is connected to every essential component of a PC. As a result, it is useful to know how to safely remove a motherboard. You might need to inspect the motherboard more closely in the event that the computer stops working properly, or you may want to replace the motherboard with one of the many different types of motherboards that are available. Regardless of the reason, removing the motherboard requires care and planning.
Outcomes	After completing this project, you will know how to: ▲ properly remove a motherboard ▲ safely store the components of the computer while removing a motherboard
What you'll need	To complete this project, you will need: ▲ an operational computer ▲ an antistatic wrist strap ▲ a technician's toolkit
Completion time	60 minutes
Precautions	Precautions similar to those from Project 3.2 apply here—whenever opening the computer's case cover, static becomes a concern.

1. First, test to see if the computer is operational. Begin by booting the computer.
2. Access all drives to verify that the computer is operational.
3. Obtain and record the CMOS hard drive information:

   _____

4. Shut down the computer.
5. Turn off the power to all peripherals that are attached to the computer.
6. Sketch the back of the computer as you disconnect all external cables.

7. Remove the computer cover.

8. Attach the anti-static wrist strap to the computer case.

9. Draw a rough sketch of the motherboard and show the location and use of each expansion slot. Sometimes an expansion card will not work if it is moved to a different slot.

_____

10. Draw a sketch of any expansion card that has wires or cables connected to it.

_____

11. Carefully add to your sketches the connection blocks and cables that attach to the expansion cards. Ribbon cables have a stripe on one edge to identify pin 1. Without this information, you may not be able to identify the connection when you reinstall the motherboard.

12. As you remove the expansion cards from the computer, disconnect all cables from them. Place the expansion cards on an antistatic mat.

13. The motherboard should now be exposed. Carefully add to your sketch the motherboard connection blocks for all cables that attach to the motherboard. For ribbon cables, note pin 1. For all other wires, be sure to show the color and function of each wire. If no distinguishing marks are available, you can use a permanent marker to make notes on the cable. Remove the power connector(s) from the motherboard, all cables to the motherboard, and any external fan connectors.

14. Remove any screws that connect the motherboard to the case (Figure 3-3).

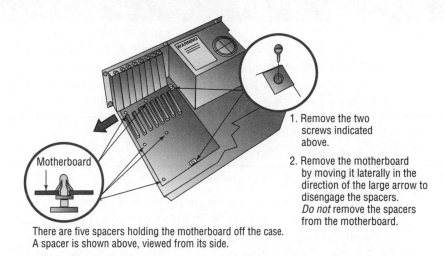

1. Remove the two screws indicated above.

2. Remove the motherboard by moving it laterally in the direction of the large arrow to disengage the spacers. *Do not* remove the spacers from the motherboard.

There are five spacers holding the motherboard off the case. A spacer is shown above, viewed from its side.

Figure 3-3: Remove the spacers and screws holding the motherboard in place

15. Remove the motherboard from the case. The plastic or brass standoffs may permit you to move the motherboard to the side and lift it out. You may have to compress the standoffs with long-nose pliers while gently lifting the system board. Use extreme care with the motherboard because bending or dropping it can easily damage it.

16. If you are not going to continue working with the motherboard, place it carefully into an anti-static bag and then into a box designed to hold it safely and securely.

Project 3.4	Installing a Motherboard
Overview	The most difficult part of motherboard removal and replacement is keeping track of what goes where. In Project 3.1, you were advised to take notes, draw diagrams, and mark wires as you removed components. Without this information, reassembly becomes a guessing game, but even with it, installing a motherboard can be a difficult procedure.
Outcomes	After completing this project, you will know how to: ▲ install a motherboard
What you'll need	To complete this project, you will need: ▲ the motherboard and computer you worked with in Project 3.3. This project assumes that the CPU, fan, and RAM chips are already installed on the motherboard ▲ the notes you took when completing Project 3.3
Completion time	60 minutes
Precautions	As always, take the necessary precautions to guard against the ESD risk from working with an open computer.

1. Remove the motherboard from its box. Leave it inside its antistatic bag and carefully place it on your work surface. Make sure you are wearing an anti-static wrist strap before taking the motherboard out of the anti-static bag. Place the motherboard on an ESD mat.
2. Open the computer case if it is not still open.
3. Locate the motherboard mounting plate (Figure 3-4).

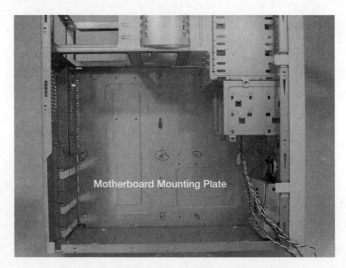

Figure 3-4: Motherboard mounting plate

4. Install plastic or brass standoffs if they are needed (Figure 3-5).

Figure 3-5: Standoffs

5. Align the keyboard connector and the expansion slots with the holes in the case (Figure 3-6).

Figure 3-6: Mounting holes

6. Secure the motherboard with the screws you removed.
7. Install the expansion cards. Use your drawings and notes to ensure that all cables and cards are installed in their original locations and are connected properly.

8. Attach the cables and internal components. ATX/NLX/ATXv12 power supply connectors connect only one way; however, if AT/Baby AT power supply cables are incorrectly connected to the motherboard, the motherboard may be damaged. The black wires on the P8 and P9 connectors are installed *black to black*.

9. Reassemble the computer.

10. Boot the computer and access all the drives to verify that the computer is operational. Does the computer boot?

Project 3.5	Identifying BIOS
Overview	The system Basic Input Output System (BIOS) controls the operation of all basic devices installed on the computer system. This makes BIOS a key component in the operation of the computer system.
	Different computer systems may have different versions of the BIOS installed. Older versions of the BIOS will not support newer devices. It is often useful to investigate which version of BIOS your computer has in order to determine whether it will be compatible with particular kinds of upgrades.
Outcomes	After completing this project, you will know how to:
	▲ determine the BIOS version currently installed on a computer
What you'll need	To complete this project, you will need:
	▲ a working computer
Completion time	30 minutes
Precautions	None

1. If necessary, shut down the computer.

2. Restart the computer by pressing the power button.

3. During the boot process, while or immediately after the computer completes the memory count (Figure 3-7), press the Pause key. Depending on the BIOS manufacturer, the F1, ESC, or DEL keys may also be used to enter the BIOS screen.

    Note that on some systems, a quiet boot option may be enabled that puts an OEM logo screen over the normal BIOS Power On Self Test (POST) screen. To see the POST screen in this configuration, press the ESC key. This will allow you to see the POST screen.

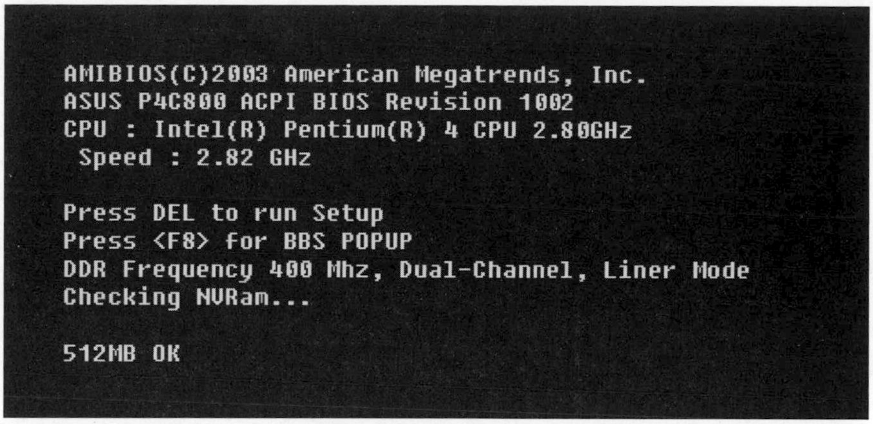

```
AMIBIOS(C)2003 American Megatrends, Inc.
ASUS P4C800 ACPI BIOS Revision 1002
CPU : Intel(R) Pentium(R) 4 CPU 2.80GHz
 Speed : 2.82 GHz


Press DEL to run Setup
Press <F8> for BBS POPUP
DDR Frequency 400 Mhz, Dual-Channel, Liner Mode
Checking NVRam...

512MB OK
```

Figure 3-7: The BIOS screen

4. The location of the BIOS publisher and BIOS ID string on screen varies depending on the vendor. Typical BIOS ID strings are long and seem random. For example, on one test system the BIOS string is: BP81010A.86A.009.P05.9911191608. Record this information for future reference.

Project 3.6	Working with Flash BIOS
Overview	Flash BIOS allows for convenient upgrading of your BIOS ROM without having to physically remove the chip. Flash BIOS is stored on a flash memory chip. This allows flashing software to change the contents of the BIOS quickly and easily. However, the process is not without important risks, so proceed with this project very carefully and only with your instructor's approval and assistance.
Outcomes	After completing this project, you will know how to: ▲ update a PC's BIOS
What you'll need	To complete this project, you will need: ▲ an operational PC ▲ a written copy of all of the configuration settings in the PC's BIOS setup files ▲ copies of the documentation for the PC's motherboard, processor, and chipset
Completion time	30 minutes

Precautions	Before beginning the project, ask your instructor if to make a full backup of the PC's hard drive just in case something goes wrong while performing this project. When flashing the BIOS ROM, be sure not to interrupt the process in any way, as interruptions can corrupt the BIOS chip quite easily. Make sure to flash the correct BIOS version, as some flash utilities will load whatever BIOS version they are given, regardless of whether it is the correct one.

1. Find the serial number and model number of the motherboard. Once you have this information, locate on the manufacturer's website the page that allows you to download the latest revisions to your PC's BIOS. Find the most current BIOS revision (usually they are listed by date and revision number) and download it. Record this information:

   _____

2. Download the latest version. You may also have to download a BIOS update utility (like `AFLASH.EXE`) if it is not included in the BIOS download.

3. If you don't already have one, either create a boot floppy using your operating system's utility or visit **www.bootdisk.com** for a boot disk for your operating system, and create a boot floppy.

4. Copy both the BIOS update (which should be something like bios.bin) and the flashing utility (something like AFLASH.exe) to this floppy disk.

5. Power on the computer, enter the BIOS Setup, and write down the boot order. Change the boot order to boot from the A: drive. Insert the floppy disk in the A: drive. Exit and save the setup.

6. Your screen should show an **A:\>** prompt. Type in the name of your flash utility executable (such as `AFLASH.EXE`) and press **Enter** to start the utility. The utility should prompt you to save a copy of your existing BIOS. You should do this in case the new BIOS is incompatible with some hardware, so you can always go back to an earlier version.

7. Flash the BIOS. Follow the instructions in the utility to start the flashing process.

   NOTE: DO NOT TURN OFF THE COMPUTER DURING THIS PROCESS! The computer may appear to not respond (for example, it may just show a flashing cursor or similar), but it is really flashing the BIOS. If you turn off your computer during the process, you won't be able to boot the computer. The only way to fix a failed flash is to send the motherboard to the manufacturer to have the BIOS chip replaced (manufacturers generally won't send out the chip as a replacement part). Let the utility flash the BIOS until it says the flash is complete. Then, follow the instructions it gives you (this usually means rebooting).

8. Verify the new BIOS. Once the flashing utility has completed, remove the floppy disk from the disk drive and reboot. You should see a new revision of the BIOS number on the boot screen. Check this against the written record you created to make sure that the flash was successful.

4

CENTRAL PROCESSING UNITS

PROJECTS

Project 4.1	Identifying a CPU
Overview	As processors have developed and advanced, features have been added that improve the performance of the processor. It is useful to understand the significance of various CPU specifications so that it is easier to know when a CPU should be upgraded. To help with this project, you will use a computer hardware configuration utility such as PC Wizard.
Outcomes	After completing this project, you will know how to: ▲ determine and analyze CPU specificiations
What you'll need	To complete this project, you will need: ▲ a working computer ▲ a utlity such as PC Wizard for identifying CPUs
Completion time	30 minutes
Precautions	None

1. Use an Internet search engine to locate and download a utility that will identify the CPU installed in a computer. Several utilities of this type are available on the Internet. If you have trouble finding one, download **PC Wizard**, which you can find at **www.cpuid.com**. While most CPU manufacturers offer such utilities in their utility download sections, they often work only for that manufacturer's CPUs. On a Windows computer, you can also find information out about the CPU installed in your computer by accessing the **System Information** dialog box via the **My Computer** window.

2. Install the utility. For instance, to install **PC Wizard**, locate the file downloaded from **www.cpuid.com** and double-click to run the file. Accept the default settings including the license agreement.

3. Run the utility either by leaving the **Run PC Wizard** option selected on the last installation screen or by double-clicking on the **PC Wizard Desktop** icon.

4. To see your computer's CPU features, click the icon representing the processor on the left menu panel.

5. **PC Wizard** displays a list of CPU features in the upper right-hand panel (Figure 4-1).

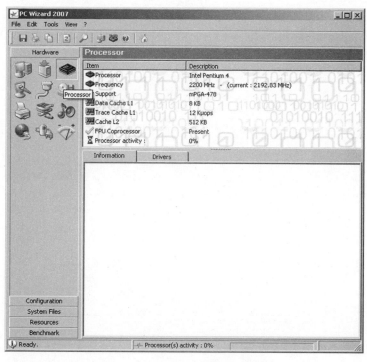

Figure 4-1: List of CPU features

6. To see more details about a feature, select an item on the list, such as **Processor** (Figure 4-2).

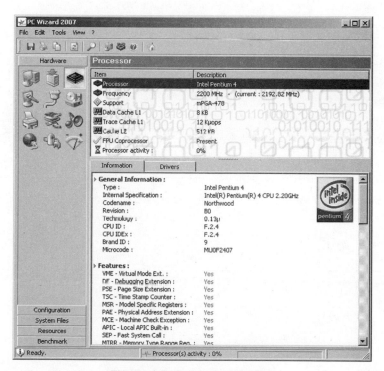

Figure 4-2: Processor details

7. Determine the following specifications for your CPU:

   Model: _____

   Technology: _____

   MMX: _____

   Streaming SIMD: _____

   SIMD Extensions 2 (SSE2): _____

   SIMD Extensions 3 (SSE3): _____

   Level 1 cache (in KB): _____

   Level 2 cache (in KB): _____

   Level 3 cache (in KB): _____

   Hyperthreading: _____

   Netburst: _____

   Burst SRAM: _____

   X86-64: _____

   Hyper pipelining: _____

   FSB frequency: _____

   Processor frequency: _____

8. If possible, repeat step 7 on an additional computer system.

   Model: _____

   Technology: _____

   MMX: _____

   Streaming SIMD: _____

   SIMD Extensions 2 (SSE2): _____

SIMD Extensions 3 (SSE3): _____

Level 1 cache (in KB): _____

Level 2 cache (in KB): _____

Level 3 cache (in KB): _____

Hyperthreading: _____

Netburst: _____

Burst SRAM: _____

X86-64: _____

Hyper pipelining: _____

FSB frequency: _____

Processor frequency: _____

9. Compare the results from the different systems. How do they differ? Which do you think is better and why?

_____

_____

_____

_____

_____

Project 4.2	Removing a CPU
Overview	Should the CPU of your computer require replacement, it will be useful to know how to remove it safely. In this project, you will gain experience with this task.
Outcomes	After completing this project, you will know how to: ▲ safely remove a computer's CPU
What you'll need	To complete this project, you will need: ▲ a computer with a CPU installed on a motherboard ▲ a technician's toolkit ▲ an antistatic wrist strap and ESD mat
Completion time	60 minutes
Precautions	This project requires you to open the computer cover. As usual, take proper precautions to guard against ESD.

1. Shut down the computer, unplug it from the power outlet, and open the computer's cover.

2. Attach your antistatic wrist strap to the metal portions of the computer case.

3. Locate the current CPU on the motherboard (see Figure 4-3).

Figure 4-3: The location of the CPU in a typical PC

4. Identify the microprocessor unit basic package type (socket or slot). Record the package type:

_____

5. If the microprocessor is a slot type microprocessor, proceed to step 10. For socket-type microprocessors, complete the following steps:

6. Carefully release the heat sink/fan assembly by raising the clip levers on opposite sides of the retention mechanism. This can be done carefully with a small flat screwdriver.

7. Detach the fan power lead from the motherboard.

8. Carefully lift the heat sink/fan assembly and remove it from the processor.

9. Modern CPU sockets use a zero insertion force (ZIF) mechanism. After the heat sink/fan assembly is removed, raise the arm lever on the processor socket to release the CPU pins and lift the CPU from its socket. Do not touch the pins on the CPU. Place the CPU on an anti-static mat.

10. For slot type microprocessors, complete the following steps:

11. Unfold the arms of the universal retention mechanism (URM) that surrounds the slot. See motherboard instructions for details. If there are latches on the arms of the URM, release them before attempting to lift the CPU. Some motherboards have clips that must be pulled back or depressed located at each end of the CPU.

12. Lift the CPU out of its slot on the motherboard. Do not touch the pins on the CPU. Detach the fan power lead from the motherboard. Place the CPU on an anti-static mat.

Project 4.3	Installing a CPU
Overview	Installing a CPU is relatively easy, although of course you still need to take care during the process not to damage the CPU pins which are extremely fragile. You must also make certain that the CPU that you are installing is compatible with the motherboard.
Outcomes	After completing this project, you will know how to: ▲ install a CPU
What you'll need	To complete this project, you will need: ▲ a new CPU, or the CPU you removed in Project 4.2 ▲ an antistatic wrist strap ▲ a technician's toolkit
Completion time	30 minutes
Precautions	This project requires you to open the computer cover. As usual, take proper precautions to guard against ESD. Also, make sure to handle the CPU with great care, as the pins are fragile and mishandling may cause serious damage.

1. Shut down the computer, unplug it from the power outlet, and open the computer's cover.

2. Locate the processor socket (Figure 4-4). The socket is a large plastic square with a square hole in the middle. It is usually white or light brown, and is surrounded by lots of small pinholes.

Figure 4-4: The processor socket on a motherboard

3. Release the locking arm (Figure 4-5). The locking arm on the left side of the socket is tucked in under a locking lip. When the arm is pushed down slightly, it releases and can be raised into an unlocked position. You may have to push the lever gently from one side to release it from its locking tabs.

Figure 4-5: The lever on a processor socket

4. Inspect the new CPU and determine which way it should be inserted. Once you have opened the socket, remove the processor from its packaging. **Note:** Be very careful not to bend any pins on the processor. You should not even touch the pins, because you may damage them. They are almost impossible to straighten properly, and if they're bent or damaged, the processor may not fit properly into the socket.

5. Determine how the CPU aligns with the socket (Figure 4-6). The processor has two sides: the side with many small pins and the top side. On the top side, notice that there is a small dot. Also notice that on the pin side, the pins are arranged in a square with two corners cut off. These cut-off corners match up with a similar pattern in the socket. There may be other locating features that help you align the processor with the socket.

Figure 4-6: Processor pin alignment with processor socket

6. At this point, the processor can be inserted into the socket (Figure 4-7).
   Note: Do not force the insertion of the processor!

Figure 4-7: Processor in place, not yet locked

7. Lower the locking arm after the processor is in place. Tuck it back under its locking lip. The processor should be locked into place (Figure 4-8).

Figure 4-8: Processor locked in place

8. Do not turn the computer back on yet, as you still need to install a heatsink, which you will do in the next project.

Project 4.4	Installing a Heatsink
Overview	Once the CPU is installed, you will need to install a cooling mechanism. Running the computer without a cooling mechanism is extremely dangerous and should never be done. Within seconds, you can permanently damage the CPU. Heatsinks are attached to the computer at mounting points on the processor using a thermal interface material, which may be thermal grease or a thermal contact patch.
Outcomes	After completing this project, you will know how to: ▲ install a heatsink
What you'll need	To complete this project, you will need: ▲ an operational computer ▲ a heatsink (with or without an attached fan) ▲ thermal grease or a thermal contact patch ▲ an antistatic wrist strap
Completion time	30 minutes
Precautions	Improper attachment of the heatsink can damage the processor, so proceed with caution as you complete this project. Use appropriate ESD measures.

1. Apply thermal grease or a thermal contact patch to the processor. Both of these items should be readily available anywhere that computer supplies are sold. If you are using a thermal compound, like grease, apply it on the small chip in the center of the CPU chip package (the processor die). If you are using a thermal contact patch, apply that in the same area. Be careful not to apply too much thermal grease; you do not need much—just a drop. You want there to be a thin layer of grease covering the entirety of the die (Figure 4-09). You don't need to spread the grease yourself—it will spread itself as you secure the heatsink.

Figure 4-9: Proper amount of thermal grease on a processor die

2. Place the heatsink over the processor socket (Figure 4-10). Make sure that the step in the bottom of the heatsink is located over the processor socket's raised portion.

Figure 4-10: The correct way of installing a CPU heatsink

3. When the heatsink is properly located, the next step is to permanently fasten it to the processor socket with a spring-loaded clamp. The clamp has two sides. One side has a small clip on it (Figure 4-11).

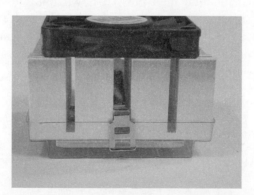

Figure 4-11: The side of a heatsink clamp with the small clip

The other side has a clip that has a tab that allows you to fit a screwdriver into it (Figure 4-12).

Figure 4-12: The other side of the heatsink clamp with the tab in the clip

4. Push the side with the small clip down and hook it under the tabs of the processor socket (Figure 4-13).

Figure 4-13: Installing the side of the heatsink clamp with the small clip

5. You will typically have to use a flat-bladed screwdriver to install the other side of the clamp. Insert the blade into the slot, and then push it down until it slides over the tab on the processor socket and locks into place (Figure 4-14). **Note:** Be careful that the heatsink doesn't move while you are doing this step. If you install the clamp and the heatsink shifts until part of it is resting on the socket, you may crack the processor package or the processor die.

Figure 4-14: Installing the other side of the heatsink clamp

6. If the heatsink you are using has an attached fan, proceed to steps 7-8. Otherwise, skip to step 9.

7. Locate the motherboard's CPU_FAN connector (Figure 4-15). This connector powers the fan for the CPU and also monitors its speed. There are usually at least two fan connectors on a typical motherboard, one for the CPU's fan and the others for other case fans, chipset fans, and so on. The CPU_FAN connector is usually white or brown and is labeled on the motherboard next to it as CPU_FAN.

Figure 4-15: A motherboard CPU_FAN connector

8. Connect the heatsink's fan wires to the motherboard using the CPU_FAN connector (Figure 4-16).

Figure 4-16: Hooking the CPU heatsink fan to the motherboard

9. Restart the computer.

10. Verify that the system recognizes the CPU by entering the BIOS setup screen and locating the CPU configuration in the CMOS settings. Be sure that the new CPU is recognized.

Project 4.5	Comparing CPUs
Overview	Shopping for CPUs can be a confusing experience. There are a vast variety of microprocessors available, and it can sometimes be difficult to determine which one is right for your computer. In this project, you will use your understanding of CPUs and their specifications to pick out a CPU that meets your specific requirements. Note that the choice of a CPU is also closely tied to the motherboard used in the system, as CPU selected must be supported by the motherboard.

Outcomes	After completing this project, you will know how to:
	▲ choose between different CPUs
What you'll need	To complete this project, you will need:
	▲ a computer with Internet access
Completion time	30 minutes
Precautions	None

1. Go online and search for 'CPU' or 'computer microprocessors'. You should be able to find an online retailer with a good selection of CPUs. You can also visit the CPUs manufacturers' website , such as Intel and AMD.

2. Pick three CPUs and gather information about them. The specifics you want to determine are as follows: processor speed, processor interface, processor class, cache size, bus speed, and the price. If some of this information is unavailable, keep searching for other products until you can gather the required information. Try to choose a mixture of different brands of CPUs for your three choices. Note that for question 5, you will need to find a CPU whose processor interface is socket 775, so at least one of the CPUs should fulfill this requirement.

CPU 1

Name: _____

Processor Speed: _____

Processor Interface: _____

Processor Class: _____

Cache Size: _____

Bus Speed: _____

Type of Heatsink/Fan Required _____

Price: _____

CPU 2

Name: _____

Processor Speed: _____

Processor Interface: _____

Processor Class: _____

Cache Size: _____

Bus Speed: _____

Type of Heatsink/Fan Required _____

Price: _____

CPU 3

Name: _____

Processor Speed: _____

Processor Interface: _____

Processor Class: _____

Cache Size: _____

Bus Speed: _____

Type of Heatsink/Fan Required _____

Price: _____

3. Assume that you are looking to buy a new computer. You want a top-end system with state-of-the-art technology across the board, since you plan to use the machine primarily for gaming. The CPU for your new system must have the highest processor speed available. Price is no object. Which of your three choices would be the best fit for you and why? Record your answer below.

_____

_____

_____

_____

4. Assume that your CPU needs replacement, but that you are happy with your current system. You want to replace your CPU with a cost-effective model that has a good bus speed for its price. You are more concerned with bus speed than any other CPU specification, including processor speed. Which of your three choices would be the best fit for you and why?

_____

_____

_____

_____

5. Assume that your CPU is malfunctioning and you are searching for appropriate replacements. You need a CPU whose processor interface is socket 775. No other processor will function with your system. Ideally, you would like to minimize the expenditure of replacing your CPU. Which of your three choices, if any, is the most appropriate for you and why?

_____

_____

_____

_____

6. Assume that you are hoping to buy an inexpensive but capable office computer for word processing, spreadsheet, and other simple tasks. You work for a small business that has a tight budget. Ideally, you would like to get a chip with a large cache size, since you plan to perform many of the same tasks repeatedly. Which of your three choices would be the best fit for you and why?

_____

_____

_____

_____

7. Assume that you are the administrator of a network of a small business. You need a computer capable of intensive database and data management. You require a system which has both top-end processor speed and top-end bus speed. Which of your three choices is the most appropriate for you and why?

_____

_____

_____

_____

5
MEMORY

Project 5.1	Identifying Memory
Overview	Before performing any complicated procedures like removing or installing memory, you should be able to quickly identify a memory module's type by observing its external features. For example, when specifications for memory modules are unavailable, you will want to be able to gain information about the module simply by looking at it. In this project, you will learn to identify memory quickly by examining the memory modules available to you.
Outcomes	After completing this project, you will know how to: ▲ identify a memory module
What you'll need	To complete this project, you will need: ▲ an uninstalled memory module, or a working computer from which you will remove a memory module ▲ an antistatic wrist strap
Completion time	30 minutes
Precautions	If you have to open up a computer to observe a memory module, take the proper precautions against ESD. Also handle the memory modules with care.

1. If necessary, connect the antistatic wrist strap to a grounded item or device. Metal case parts on the back of a grounded computer provide this ground connection.

2. If necessary, determine if the module is SIMM, DIMM, or RIMM (Figure 5-1). Examine the number of pins and the position of notches to help determine which memory module type you have. Record the number of pins and the module type:

    Pins: _____

    Type: _____

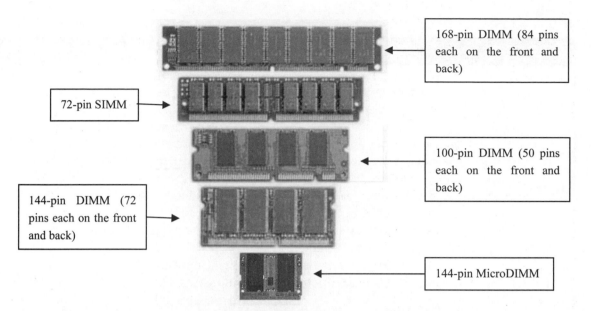

Figure 5-1: DRAM form factors

3. Carefully observe any labels on the memory module. These labels may be stickers or printed directly on the module and memory chips. Record the information from the labels.

_____

4. Try to determine the RAM speed (frequency).
   a. On SIMM modules, look for a number (such as 6) on the end of a number. This number, multiplied by 10, indicates the nanosecond speed rating of the module.
   b. On DIMM and RIMM modules, look for a number following the letters PC (such as PC133). This number indicates the frequency of the memory module or the number of megabytes transferred per second to and from the memory module.
5. Record the RAM speed of your module:

   Speed: _____

6. Determine if the module includes error detection and/or correction (ECC). Count the number of chips on the module and then divide by 3. If the result is a whole number, the module is most probably either parity or error correction code (ECC) memory. Record your result.

_____

7. Record the results of your observations to indicate the type of memory module. For example, a SIMM that uses parity/ECC and has the number 6 as a part of the number should be recorded as SIMM 60 as error detecting.

_____

8. If additional modules are available, repeat this process.

Project 5.2	Examining Memory Areas
Overview	Managing memory in early PCs and operating systems was a complex task. For the purposes of interacting with software, early operating systems such as Windows 9x divided system memory logically into sections. The first 640KB of the first megabyte of RAM (known as conventional memory) was used for configuring the DOS program environment The rest of the first megabyte of RAM (640 KB—1024 KB), (called upper memory), was reserved for the computer's needs, such as for the system BIOS and device drivers. The area above 1 MB was referred to as expanded memory, with the first 64 K of the second megabyte called the high memory area. The high memory area could be accessed in real mode (i.e., directly contacted by applications) while the area above it was used for programs and data running in protected mode (in which the operating system acts as an interface between RAM and applications).
	Subsequent Windows operating systems (starting with Windows NT and including Windows 2000, Windows XP, Windows Vista, and Window Server 2003) dispensed with support for real mode and the distinctions between different types of memory. Instead all memory is treated as the same block of memory and is managed by the operating system's memory manager.
	One of the features of protected mode is the ability to use virtual memory. With virtual memory the operating system uses spare hard drive space as a temporary memory storage area in addition to the system memory. This substantially increases your machine's effective memory—even though disk-based memory is noticeably slower than chip-based memory. The virtual memory space on a hard disk is called either a page file or a swap file, depending on the version of Windows you're running and access to memory is controlled by the operating systems memory manager. Current Windows operating systems all use virtual memory.
	The Windows Task Manager provides information about programs and processes running on a Windows 2000/XP/Vista computer. The following are categories of memory displayed by the Task Manager:
	• **Total Physical Memory:** the total RAM installed in the computer.
	• **Available Physical Memory:** the portion of installed RAM that is not allocated to a program or process.
	• **Commit Charge:** memory allocated to programs and processes. The Commit Charge may be larger than the total physical memory because it includes used virtual memory.
	• **Kernel Memory:** memory used by the operating system.
	• **Handles:** value that indicates the number of object handles (instructions handled).

	• **Threads:** objects that run program instructions. Threads allow more than one program instruction to be run at one time. • **Processes:** tasks that are currently active. • **System Cache:** the current physical memory used to map pages of open files. • **Paged Memory:** memory used in the paging process. Paging is the process of moving infrequently used parts of a program from RAM to a storage medium. • **Non-Paged Memory:** operating system memory that is never paged to disk. In this project, you will use utilities provided by Windows to gain a better understanding of a system's memory and how to manage it.
Outcomes	After completing this project, you will know how to: ▲ examine a system's memory on a Windows 2000 or Windows XP computer
What you'll need	To complete this project, you will need: ▲ a computer with Windows XP or Windows 2000 installed
Completion time	60 minutes
Precautions	None

1. To use the **System Information** utility to examine memory resources, open the **Start** menu, point to **All Programs**, point to **Accessories**, point to **System Tools** and then click **System Information** (Figure 5-2).

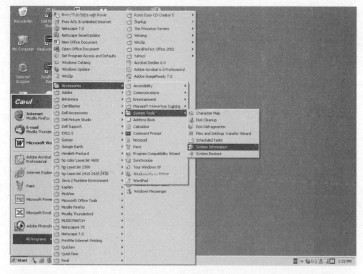

Figure 5-2: Accessing the System Information dialog box

2. The **System Information** utility will open. Select the **System Summary** and record the following information:

Total Physical Memory: _____

Available Physical Memory: _____

Total Virtual Memory: _____

Available Virtual Memory: _____

Page File Space: _____

Note: You can print the information available in the utility by opening the **View** menu and selecting the **Print** command.

3. In the **System Information** dialog box, click the plus sign by **Hardware Resources** to open the **Hardware** tree. In the **Hardware** tree, click **I/O** and record the I/O address (I/O Range) used by **COM 1**.

4. Click **Memory** (Figure 5-3) and record the memory addresses used by the system board.

_____

_____

_____

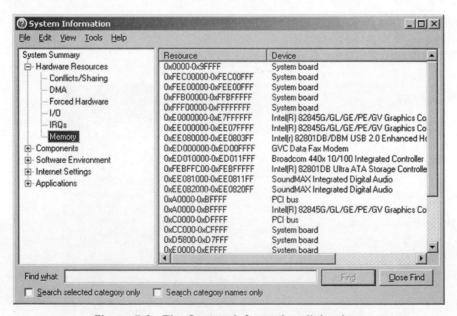

Figure 5-3: The System Information dialog box

5. Click **Conflicts/Sharing** and list any memory addresses that are shared.

_____

_____

_____

6. Now you will use the **Task Manager** to examine memory. To open the **Task Manager**, right-click the **Taskbar** and select **Task Manager**.

7. Click the **Performance** tab (Figure 5-4) and record the following information

CPU Usage: _____

Paged File Usage (or PF Usage): _____

Physical Memory (Total): _____

Physical Memory (Available): _____

Commit Charge Total: _____

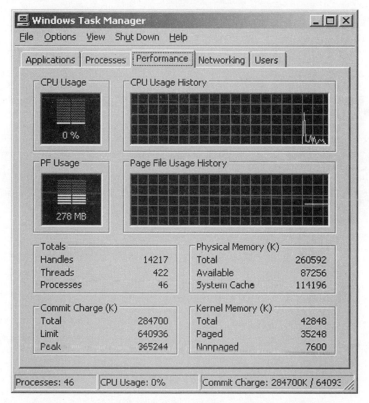

Figure 5-4: The Performance tab in the Task Manager

8. Without closing the **Task Manager**, open the **Paint** program by opening the **Start** menu, pointing to **All Programs**, pointing to **Accessories**, and then clicking **Paint**.

9. Without closing the **Paint** program, open the **Control Panel**.

10. You should now have the **Task Manager**, the **Paint** program, and **Control Panel** running. Record the following information:

    CPU Usage: _____

    Paged Usage: _____

    Physical Memory Total: _____

    Physical Memory Available: _____

    Commit Charge Total: _____

    When you compare the values you recorded in Step 10 with the values you recorded in Step 7, you should find that opening the two tasks caused an increase in resource usage. If the usage exceeds 70 percent, the computer is likely to have difficulty.

11. Click the **Applications** tab in the **Task Manager** and record the displayed tasks below.

    _____

    _____

    _____

12. Click the **Processes** tab in the **Task Manager** and record the memory usage of the **Paint** program (**MSPAINT.EXE**).

    _____

13. Evaluate the PC that you used to record your findings Do you think the PC is operating as efficiently and speedily as it could? Does it need more RAM. Why or why not?

    _____

    _____

    _____

Project 5.3	Removing Memory
Overview	There are may possible situations in which you might need to install new memory in your computer. Before you can do this, however, you will need to know how to remove the existing memory module properly. As always, correctly removing a component of the computer requires care and planning, but memory is one of the simpler components of the computer to remove and install.
Outcomes	After completing this project, you will know how to: ▲ examine memory areas in Windows 2000 or Windows XP
What you'll need	To complete this project, you will need: ▲ an operational computer ▲ an antistatic wrist strap and ESD mat ▲ a technician's toolkit
Completion time	60 minutes
Precautions	As always, take the necessary precautions to guard against ESD risk from working with an open computer, and handle memory modules with care.

1. If necessary, shut down the computer and disconnect it from the power outlet.
2. Attach the antistatic wrist strap to a metal portion of the computer case.
3. Explain why it is necessary to wear an antistatic wrist strap for this project.

_____

4. Open the case and remove the cover.
5. Locate the memory modules in the computer (Figure 5-5).

Figure 5-5: Location of memory within a system

6. What type of memory modules are installed: SIMM, DIMM, or RIMM (see Project 5.1)?

_____

7. If the modules are:

   a. SIMM, release the spring clips from both ends that hold the module in place (Figure 5-6).

   b. DIMM or RIMM, push the tabs (catches) out from both ends of the module to release the module.

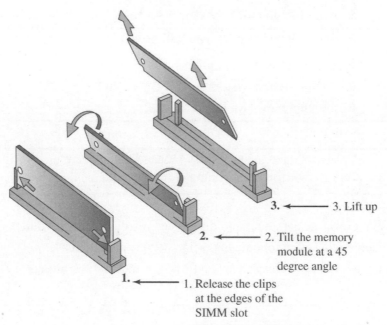

3. ← 3. Lift up

2. ← 2. Tilt the memory module at a 45 degree angle

1. ← 1. Release the clips at the edges of the SIMM slot

Figure 5-6: Removing a SIMM

8. Carefully remove the module(s) from the computer and set aside on an anti-static mat.

Project 5.4	Installing Memory
Overview	Once your old memory has been removed, the next step is to replace it with a new module. This can be a tricky process due to the different kinds of memory modules. You will need to be able to correctly identify the new module as well as its proper placement on the motherboard. Once again, when working with an open computer, take the necessary precautions to guard against ESD.
Outcomes	After completing this project, you will know how to: ▲ install a memory module
What you'll need	To complete this project, you will need: ▲ a new memory module for installation (or, alternatively, the memory you removed in Project 5.3 ▲ an antistatic wrist strap
Completion time	60 minutes
Precautions	As always, take the necessary precautions to guard against ESD risk from working with an open computer and handle the memory modules with care.

1. Determine the slot order for module installation. Generally, it is best to install modules in reverse order from how previous modules were removed. If more modules will be installed than were removed, it may be necessary to install modules in previously empty memory slots before filling the previously used memory slots. In some instances, it may be necessary to temporarily remove an interface card to allow enough room to release the tabs (catches) on a memory slot.

2. Remove the module from the antistatic packaging.

3. If the module is a:

    a. DIMM or RIMM, place the module into the slot and gently push down on the module while pushing in on the catches at each end of the slot.

    b. SIMM, place the module into the slot on a 45° angle. Then gently push the memory module up into a vertical position until catches on each end hold the module into place.

4. After all modules have been installed, test the computer to be certain that it is working correctly and that it recognizes all the installed memory.

    a. Detach the antistatic strap from the computer.

    b. Reattach the computer to external power.

    c. Power on the computer and observe the startup process.

5. The computer should count all of the newly installed RAM and properly load the operating system. Once the operating system has loaded, you can use open the **My Computer** window to access the **System Properties** dialog box's **General** tab to check the amount of installed memory (Figure 5-7). Record the amount of installed memory.

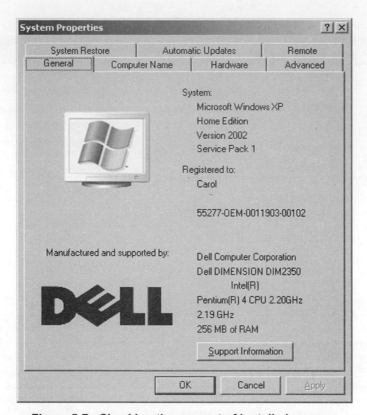

Figure 5-7: Checking the amount of installed memory

6. If the computer does not boot properly, or your newly installed memory is not recognized, shut down the computer, unplug the power cord from the power outlet, and repeat Steps 3 and 4. If the computer still does not boot properly, make sure that you are using the right type of memory module, and you are not trying to install more memory than your computer can support. If it does, and you still cannot successfully install the memory after repeated attempts, the memory module may be defective, and you should retry with a different module.

Project 5.5	Comparing Memory Modules
Overview	Installing new memory modules can be useful in many situations. For example, when an older computer needs extra resources to handle a new, complicated program or you want to upgrade the computer's operating system, the computer's memory might need to be upgraded. Perhaps some portion of the memory has become unreadable and needs to be replaced. Whatever the reason, it will be useful for you to be able to use the specifications of memory modules to determine an appropriate choice given a particular situation. In this exercise, you will use the Internet to find and compare several different memory modules.
Outcomes	After completing this project, you will know how to: ▲ choose appropriate memory modules given different sets of circumstances
What you'll need	To complete this project, you will need: ▲ a computer with Internet access
Completion time	30 minutes
Precautions	None

1. Perform a web search for RAM or 'memory upgrade'. Find an online retailer with a good selection of different kinds of RAM. **Crucial.com** and **Memory.com** are also a good sources of information on memory upgrades.

2. Determine the minimum and recommended memory requirements for the following operating systems:

   Windows Vista: _____

   Windows XP: _____

   Windows 2000: _____

   Macintosh OS X: _____

   Red Hat Linux with an Intel CPU: _____

3. Choose three memory modules and record the following information: memory size, memory speed, memory type, number of pins, and price.

Memory Module 1

Memory size: _____

Memory speed: _____

Memory type: _____

Number of pins: _____

Price: _____

Memory Module 2

Memory size: _____

Memory speed: _____

Memory type: _____

Number of pins: _____

Price: _____

Memory Module 3

Memory size: _____

Memory speed: _____

Memory type: _____

Number of pins: _____

Price: _____

4. Assume that the marketing department of your company has decided to purchase a new program to help automate its marketing tasks. The chief technical officer has asked you to investigate the computer systems to help determine what additional requirements might be necessary to use the new application. Although other requirements of the application seem standard, you notice that the application places heavy memory requirements on the computer systems. Which of your three choices would be most appropriate and why?

_____

_____

_____

_____

5. Assume that you are interested in upgrading the memory of a computer you use primarily for gaming. The amount of memory is important to you, but not nearly as much as speed. You want the fastest memory module you can find. Which of your three choices would be most appropriate and why?

_____

_____

_____

_____

6. Assume that your computer has recently been generating error messages concerning a lack of available memory. You want to replace your memory as soon as you can. You use your computer for simple tasks like using the Internet and word processing. Ideally, you would find the least expensive memory module that still offers you decent performance and reliability. Which of your three choices would be most appropriate and why?

_____

_____

_____

_____

6
BUS STRUCTURES

PROJECTS

Project 6.1	PC Bus Architectures (Identifying Expansion Slots)
Overview	A bus is a set of signal pathways that allow data to travel inside or outside the computer. Computers have internal buses (inside the microprocessor) and external buses (outside the microprocessor). In this project, we will explore external buses and expansion slots for peripheral devices. The expansion bus (slot) provides power (+5 volts, +12 volts, and ground), the data bus allows for information exchange, the address bus provides access to memory, and the control bus is used for clock signals and IRQ signals.
Outcomes	After completing this project, you will know how to: ▲ identify components of external bus architecture
What you'll need	To complete this project, you will need: ▲ a technician's toolkit, including anti-static wrist strap ▲ a computer that you can take apart; or alternatively, a motherboard
Completion time	30 minutes
Precautions	This project requires opening the computer cover, so take the proper steps to guard against ESD.

1. If necessary, shut down the computer and disconnect it from any external power. **Note**: If you are using a motherboard that has already been removed from a computer, skip to Step 4.

2. Carefully remove the system case cover and attach your antistatic wrist strap to a metal portion of the computer case.

3. If it is necessary to disconnect any cables during this project, take notes and carefully sketch where they were originally connected.

4. Locate the expansion slots on the motherboard.

5. Does the motherboard include ISA expansion slots? If so, record the total number of ISA slots (Figure 6-1) as well as the number of empty ISA slots:

   Total ISA slots: _____

   Empty ISA slots: _____

Figure 6-1: ISA slots

6. Does the motherboard include PCI slots? If so, record the total number of PCI slots (Figure 6-2), as well as the number of empty PCI slots.

    Total PCI slots: _____

    Empty PCI slots: _____

Figure 6-2: PCI expansion slots

7. If the motherboard has both ISA and PCI slots, count and record the combined number of ISA and PCI slots and the number of expansion brackets on the back of the computer:

_____

8. If there are more slots than brackets, the ISA and PCI slots that are adjacent are a "shared" slot. This means that you can install a card in the ISA slot or the PCI slot of this pair, but you may not install a card in both the ISA and the adjacent PCI slot. Is this the case with the system you are working on?

_____

9. Does the motherboard include an AGP slot (Figure 6-3)?

_____

Figure 6-3: AGP slot compared to a PCI slot

10. Does the motherboard include a PCIe (PCI Express) expansion slot?

_____

11. After you have located each type of slot on your motherboard, make a drawing of the board and its bus expansion slots. Label each bus expansion slot with its bus type, bus width in bits, and bus speed in MHz. Use the space below for your sketch or draw on a separate piece of paper.

_____

12. List the buses found that support bus mastering.

_____

_____

13. Record the name of the chipset.

_____

14. If you disconnected any cards or cables during this project, use your notes and sketch to carefully reconnect them.

15. Disconnect the antistatic wrist strap from the computer case and reattach the power cord to the computer's power supply.

16. Plug the computer in to an external power source and turn it to test any components that were disconnected during this project.

17. Replace and secure the case cover.

Project 6.2	Reviewing System Resources
Overview	The four system resources are I/O addresses, IRQs, DMA (direct memory access) channels, and memory addresses. An interrupt request (IRQ) is a request from a device to the CPU for a service, action, or special action. Each device is assigned a specific IRQ number so that the processor knows the device to which it must respond. Two devices can share an IRQ number, but if both devices are active at any time the CPU may send its responses to the wrong device, causing serious errors. You will need to be able to resolve conflicts between devices that Windows cannot resolve by itself. In this project, you will practice this task by accessing the Device Manager and System Information utility and examining your system resources.
Outcomes	After completing this project, you will know how to: ▲ use the Device Manager and System Information utility to resolve system resource conflicts
What you'll need	To complete this project, you will need: ▲ a computer with Windows XP or Windows 2000 installed
Completion time	60 minutes
Precautions	None

■ Part A: Using the Device Manager

1. In **Windows 2000**, open the **Control Panel** and then click the **System** applet to open the **Device Manager**. In **Windows XP**, right-click **My Computer** and select **Properties** to open the **System Properties** dialog box (alternatively, you can open the **Control Panel** and click **System** to open the **Systems Properties** dialog box). Choose the **Hardware** tab, and then click the **Device Manager** button to open the **Device Manager**.

2. Open the **View** menu and select **Resources by Type**.

3. Click the expand button (+) in front of **Interrupt Request (IRQ)** to expand the list of IRQ assignments (Figure 6-4).

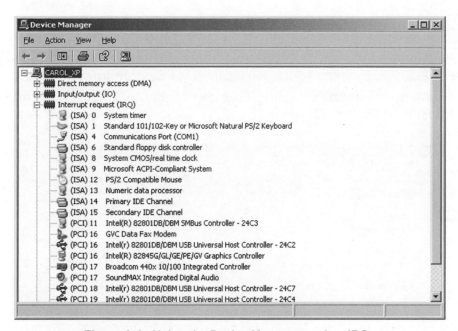

Figure 6-4: Using the Device Manager to view IRQs

4. Record the IRQs you see listed:

_____

_____

_____

_____

_____

_____

_____

_____

_____

5. Click on the expand buttons in front of **Direct Memory Access (DMA)** and **Input/Output (I/O)** to view other resources, such as DMA assignments.

6. Locate the system resources (IRQ, DMA, I/O, and memory if applicable) for a standard floppy controller. Record this information:

IRQ: _____

DMA: _____

I/O: _____

Memory: _____

■ Part B: Using the System Information utility

1. Open the **Start** menu, point to **Programs** (or **All Programs** for **Windows XP**), then **Accessories**, then **System Tools**, and finally select **System Information**.

2. In the **System Information** utility, click the expand button (+) next to **Hardware Resources** in the left pane (Figure 6-5).

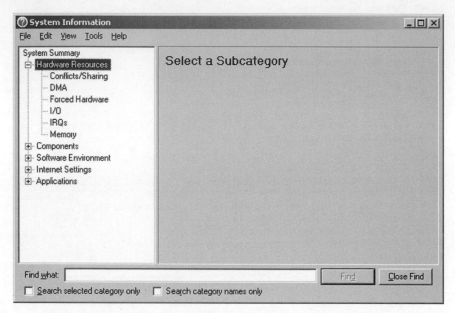

Figure 6-5: Hardware Resources in the System Information utility

3. You should see the following listed under **Hardware Resources**:
   - Conflicts/Sharing
   - DMA
   - Forced Hardware
   - I/O
   - IRQs
   - Memory

4. To review the current assignments for system resources, such as resources that are conflicting or shared (Conflicts/Sharing), or any hardware configured manually instead of using **Plug and Play** (Forced Hardware), select these options under **Hardware** in the left pane. Record what you see.

---

5. Using **System Information**, locate the system resources currently assigned to the keyboard. Record what you find.

_____

_____

_____

_____

_____

_____

Project 6.3	Installing a Legacy Expansion Card
Overview	An expansion card is a circuit board that you install into a computer to increase its capabilities. They include a connector and a metal tab that holds ports or adapters. There are different kinds of expansion cards, and each kind must be installed in the corresponding expansion slot on the motherboard. In this project, you will gain experience working with installing an expansion card that is not Plug and Play-compatible (a legacy device). These devices are gradually being replaced with Plug and Play versions, which are far more convenient, but it is still useful to know how to install an older card, or a card on a legacy system, that is not Plug and Play-compatible.
Outcomes	After completing this project, you will know how to: ▲ install an expansion card that is not Plug and Play-compatible
What you'll need	To complete this project, you will need: ▲ a technician's toolkit, including an anti-static wrist strap ▲ an expansion card that is not Plug and Play-compatible, such as an ISA modem card, and its device driver ▲ a computer in which to install the expansion card ▲ if the card has jumper or switch settings that need to be manually set, you will need the manual for the computer to do so
Completion time	30 minutes
Precautions	This project requires opening the computer cover, so take the proper steps to guard against ESD.

■ Part A: Install an expansion card that is not Plug and Play-compatible

1. If necessary, shut down the computer and disconnect the power cable from the back of the computer.

2. Remove the cover from the computer case and connect the antistatic wrist strap to a metal portion of the computer case.

3. Search the card for manual jumper or switch settings. Using the jumpers or switches on the card, set its IRQ, I/O, and DMA addresses. **Note**: You need the computer's manual to do this.

4. Locate an available ISA slot in the computer system.

5. Remove the bracket from the back of the computer to make room for the device.

6. Carefully insert the card into the open ISA slot.

7. Place a system case screw into the bracket to hold the card in place.

8. Disconnect your antistatic wrist strap and reattach the computer's power cord.

■ Part B: Install the device driver for the new card in Windows 2000/XP

1. Boot and log on to the computer.

2. **Windows 2000** and **Windows XP** automatically detect new Plug and Play hardware at startup. If the system detects your ISA device, skip to Step 13.

3. Open the **Control Panel**. In **Windows 2000**, select **Add New Hardware** to open the **Add Hardware Wizard**. (In **Windows XP**, select **Phone and Modem Options** in the **Control Panel**. In the **Phone and Modem** dialog box, select the **Modems** tab, and click Add to open the **Add Hardware Wizard.**)

4. The **Wizard** will ask you if you want Windows to detect the new modem card (Figure 6-6). Click Next.

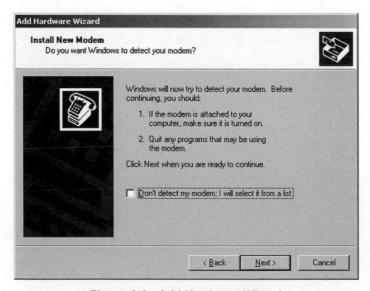

Figure 6-6: Add Hardware Wizard

5. At this point, Windows will attempt to detect the new modem. If it cannot find it, click Next to select the modem from a list (Figure 6-7).

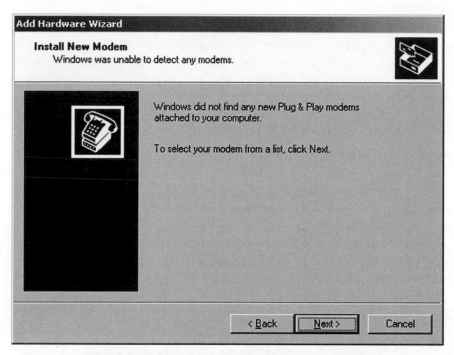

Figure 6-7: New Plug and Play Modem Not Found

6. On the next screen of the **Wizard**, you can select the manufacturer and model of the modem, or, if the modem is not listed or you have the device driver for the modem on a disk, use the Have Disk button (Figure 6-8). Place the disk with the device driver in the disk drive and select the Have Disk button.

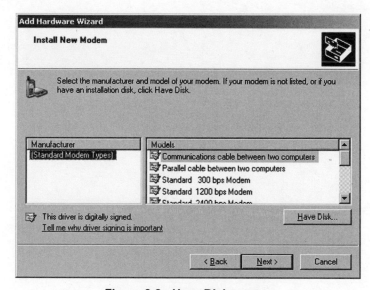

Figure 6-8: Have Disk screen

7. If necessary, browse to the correct drive and folder that contains the device driver. Select the Driver file and click OK.

8. Windows loads the appropriate driver files for the device from the driver diskette. After the files are loaded, Windows displays any required additional screens to complete the configuration. In the case of the modem, Windows may prompt you to select the communications port associated with the modem. Select the communications port that you manually configured on the modem card and answer the questions as required.

9. When the device installation is complete, Windows displays a screen stating that the device has been successfully installed. Select Finish. In some cases it may be necessary to restart the computer to activate the newly installed ISA device.

10. After restarting the PC, test the legacy device. To test the modem, open the **Start** menu, point to **All Programs**, open the **Control Panel**, double-click **Modems**, and select the modem to open the modem's **Properties** dialog box. On the **Advanced** tab, click **Diagnostics**. If the device is not working, verify all settings including those configured using jumpers or switches on the device. If and when the problem is located and corrected, retest the device. After the device is working correctly, replace the system case cover.

Project 6.4	Installing Plug and Play Expansion Cards
Overview	The majority of computers today are compatible with Plug and Play. In this project, you will use a PCI modem adapter card to help you gain experience installing Plug and Play expansion cards. Because Plug and Play is more efficient for installing new cards, this task should be simpler than installing a legacy expansion card. If a PCI modem adapter card is unavailable, there are many other alternatives for Plug and Play expansion cards that you can practice with, but some of the steps below may not apply.
Outcomes	After completing this project, you will know how to: ▲ install a Plug and Play expansion card
What you'll need	To complete this project, you will need: ▲ a technician's toolkit, including an anti-static wrist strap ▲ a PCI modem adapter card ▲ a Plug and Play-compatible computer system
Completion time	30 minutes
Precautions	This project requires opening the computer cover, so take the proper steps to guard against ESD.

■ Part A: Install a Plug and Play expansion card

1. Read the manual for the PCI modem adapter. Some PCI modems want you to install the software driver first. If this is the case, install the software that came with the PCI modem.
2. If necessary, shut down the computer and disconnect the power cable from the back of the computer.
3. Carefully remove the case cover and connect the antistatic wrist strap to a metal portion of the computer case.
4. Locate an empty PCI slot on the motherboard.
5. Remove the bracket from the computer case.
6. Carefully insert the PCI modem adapter card into the open PCI slot.
7. Attach the PCI modem adapter card using a computer case screw.
8. Remove the antistatic wrist strap and reattach the power cord to the computer system.
9. Boot and log on to the computer.
10. **Windows 2000/Windows XP** detects new Plug and Play hardware at startup. This process should detect the PCI modem adapter and launch the **Add New Hardware Wizard**.
11. The wizard should detect the device and list the device by type, name, and model .

12. After selecting next, the wizard prompts you for the location of the device drivers. Select the **Search for the best driver for your device** option button and click Next (Figure 6-9).

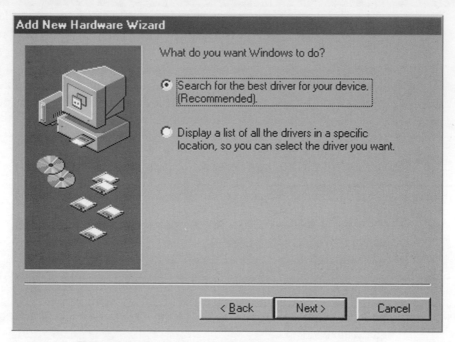

Figure 6-9: Search for the best driver for your device

13. The wizard now displays a list of locations that Windows will search for the proper device driver, including the operating system driver database. To narrow the search, select the floppy drive, CD-ROM drive and/or Specify Location (browse to the location) option buttons depending on the location of the drivers you have on disk. The wizard will select the best driver either on the disk or from the operating system driver database. After making the selections for driver locations, click Next (Figure 6-10).

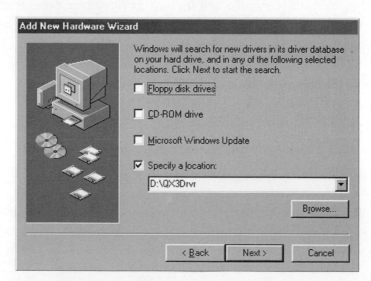

Figure 6-10: Select the location of the driver

14. The wizard displays the driver selected. If you are not satisfied with the selection, use the back button to return to previous screens. If the driver selected is acceptable, click **Next** (Figure 6-11).

Figure 6-11: Select the driver

15. The wizard completes the installation of the device drivers and displays a dialog box indicating that the device installation is complete. Click Finish (Figure 6-12).

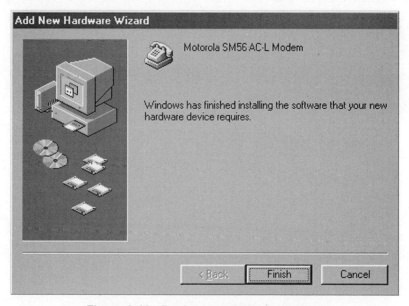

Figure 6-12: Device installation complete

16. Test the PCI modem by connecting the modem to a working phone line.

17. Configure a communications package to utilize the newly installed modem and have that package dial an ISP.

18. When the modem dials successfully and connects, the modem has been successfully installed.

Project 6.5	Comparing Buses
Overview	In many cases, you will be asked to recommend a motherboard with particular bus specifications that are suited for various tasks. In this project, you will use your knowledge of bus specifications to recommend appropriate motherboards for different scenarios.
Outcomes	After completing this project, you will know how to: ▲ compare buses and use bus specifications to pick motherboards appropriately
What you'll need	To complete this project, you will need: ▲ a computer with Internet access
Completion time	30 minutes
Precautions	None

1. Perform a web search for 'motherboards'. Find an online retailer with a good selection of different motherboards. If you can't find one, try Tiger Direct or CDW.

2. Choose three motherboards and record the following information: front side bus speed (if more than one speed is listed, list both speeds), number of PCI and/or PCIe expansion slots, number of AGP expansion slots, AGP speed, number of USB ports, and price.

Motherboard 1

Front side bus speed: _____

Number of PCI expansion slots: _____

Number of PCIe expansion slots:_____

Lane width of of PCIe slots: _____

Number of AGP expansion slots: _____

AGP speed: _____

Number of USB ports: _____

Number of serial ATA headers: _____

Price: _____

Motherboard 2

Front side bus speed: _____

Number of PCI expansion slots: _____

Number of PCIe expansion slots: _____

Lane width of of PCIe slots: _____

Number of AGP expansion slots: _____

AGP speed: _____

Number of USB ports: _____

Number of serial ATA headers: _____

Price: _____

Motherboard 3

Front side bus speed: _____

Number of PCI expansion slots: _____

Number of PCIe expansion slots: _____

Lane width of of PCIe slots: _____

Number of AGP expansion slots: _____

AGP speed: _____

Number of USB ports: _____

Number of serial ATA headers: _____

Price: _____

3. Assume that you are the network administrator for a small business. You need a computer that can function as a server for the business. Since you will be using the computer to stream video over the Internet, you would like something equipped with as many serial ATA headers as you can find so that you can speed up your transfer rates. The system will also need to have a large number of USB ports. Which of your three choices would be most appropriate and why?

    _____

    _____

    _____

    _____

4. Assume that you are interested in buying a computer you will use primarily for gaming. You know that you will want to have a motherboard with AGP slots and as much AGP speed as you can find. Price is no object. Which of your three choices would be most appropriate and why?

    _____

    _____

    _____

    _____

5. Assume that you are in the market for a new home computer. You use your computer for simple tasks like using the Internet and word processing. While you don't want a system that is outdated, you don't want to spend a lot on your new system. Which of your three choices would be most appropriate and why?

    _____

    _____

    _____

    _____

    _____

7

HARD DRIVES

PROJECTS

Project 7.1	Examining Drive Geometry
Overview	To understand how disks store data, you need to understand disk geometry, which refers to the electronic organization of the disk drive. The components of disk geometry include the physical number of read/write heads (usually one for each side of the platter), and the number of cylinders, tracks, and sectors of the disk. You can use this information to determine the storage capacity of a hard drive. In this project, you will examine the drive geometry (cylinders, heads, and sectors) of a hard drive. Older drives list the cylinders, heads, and sectors (or the sectors per track—SPT). (Note that because the number of tracks per surface is the same as the number of cylinders on the drive, manufacturers only report the number of cylinders, not tracks.)
Outcomes	After completing this project, you will know how to: ▲ identify the drive geometry of a hard drive ▲ use drive geometry information to calculate the available data storage space on the drive
What you'll need	To complete this project, you will need: ▲ an older IDE hard drive that lists the cylinders, heads, and sectors, and which has already been removed from the computer ▲ a calculator
Completion time	30 minutes
Precautions	On newer drives (generally those that can store over 8.4 GB), the drive will list the mode, such as LBA (Logical Block Addressing) and the number of hard drive sectors. For such hard drives, you cannot use the below steps to calculate storage capacity.

1. Examine the hard drive to locate a section labeled Parameters (Figure 7-1).

Figure 7-1: Locating the Parameters section on a hard drive

2. Enter the information you find:

    Cylinders: _____

    Heads: _____

    Sectors: _____

3. Calculate drive geometry using the formula: Cylinders x Heads x Sectors x 512 = Drive Capacity.

    _____

4. Convert the result above into MB by dividing by 1,000,000 or into GB by dividing by 1,000,000,000.

    _____

5. What is the storage capacity of the drive?

    _____

6. What is the storage capacity of a drive with the following drive geometry: 15690 cylinders, 16 heads and 63 sectors per track.

Project 7.2	Removing an IDE Hard Drive
Overview	IDE (Integrated Device Electronics) is an interface for connecting storage devices such as hard drives, tape drives and optical (CD/DVD) drives. IDE is a specification that was originally written in 1988. When it was accepted as an ANSI standard, it was renamed Advanced Technology Attachment (ATA). The first ATA standards used a parallel bus, and are referred to as parallel ATA or PATA. The most recent ATA standards are based on a serial bus and referred to as serial ATA (SATA). IDE has been the most popular interface for hard disk drives in mainstream systems for many years, which means that you will very likely be called upon to remove and install them. In this project, you will identify and remove an IDE hard drive.
Outcomes	After completing this project, you will know how to: ▲ identify an IDE hard drive ▲ remove an IDE hard drive
What you'll need	To complete this project, you will need: ▲ working Windows computer with an IDE hard drive installed ▲ a technician's toolkit with antistatic wrist strap and antistatic mat
Completion time	60 minutes
Precautions	Be sure to take all necessary ESD precautions. Also make sure that any data on the hard drive that you will be removing has been backed up.

1. If necessary, turn on the computer, and access the CMOS setup routine (also referred to as the BIOS setup program or BIOS screen). The CMOS setup routine is available for only a short time during the book sequence. Most computer manufacturers tell you how to enter the CMOS startup screen as the computer is booting, typically by pressing a specific key combination, such as F2 or Ctrl +F1. The initial screen typically displays a menu of configuration categories, each of which lead to one or more additional menu screens and options (Figure 7-2). Select the **Drive Configuration** option and press the Enter key. Record the information that appears.

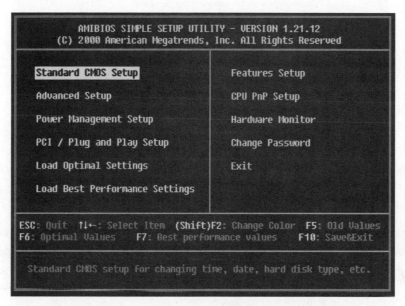

Figure 7-2: Accessing the CMOS setup routine

2. When you have finished recording the information, press the Escape key and allow the computer to finish booting.

3. Shut down the computer and disconnect the power cable, along with any external peripheral cables.

4. Carefully remove the computer case. **Note:** As soon as the cover is removed, put on your antistatic wrist strap to protect the computer from ESD.

5. Prepare a sketch that shows where each expansion card goes in the motherboard expansion slots and where any cables or wires are connected to the expansion card. On this sketch, note the pin 1 edge (the edge that has a stripe) on the cables and the colors of individual wires attached to the expansion card.

6. If any of the expansion cards are obstructing your access to the hard drive, you will need to remove them. Disconnect the wires and cables that are connected to the expansion card, remove the mounting screw, grasp the expansion card with both hands, and pull upward while gently rocking the board from front to back (Figure 7-3). **Note:** As soon as the expansion card is out, place it on an antistatic mat to protect against ESD.

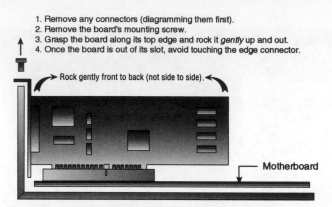

Figure 7-3: Removing the expansion card

7. The power cable plug on the hard drive is keyed so it fits only one way, but the ribbon (data) cable can be accidentally reversed if it is not keyed. To keep this from happening, note the pin 1 position of the hard drive so you can later match it with the striped edge on the data cable when the drive is reinstalled. After you've done this, disconnect the data cable (ribbon cable) and power cable from the hard drive.

8. Physically remove the hard drive from the computer. Unbolt the hard drive from the drive bay and then remove the drive from the computer.

9. In another sketch, draw the hard-drive jumper block and show the current jumper settings.

Note: The jumper settings should be master or single if this is the bootable drive. If the jumper settings do not match the installation, the drive will not function. Hard drive jumpers found in various locations on hard drives set the installation options. If any hard drive jumper is moved, the hard-drive configuration is changed. Sometimes it is very difficult to find documentation for jumper settings. Hard drives may be configured as master, single, slave, or cable select. The hard-drive configuration must match the drive's usage. The cable select status permits the computer to automatically select the master or slave status, but it requires a special hard-drive cable that is identified by a notch or hole in the cable.

Project 7.3	Installing an IDE Hard Drive
Overview	Before installing a new IDE hard drive, you will need to plan how it will be configured. IDE drives are connected to the motherboard using an IDE ribbon cable. Motherboards typically have two connectors for IDE ribbon cables, called the primary IDE channel and the secondary IDE channel. The IDE ribbon cables themselves have a connector for attaching to the motherboard and one or two connectors for the IDE drives. If two drives are connected with the same ribbon cable, one drive must be designated as Master and one as Slave. This configuration is done typically through jumpers or switches on the drive itself. Other drive configuration options include Single, which specifies that there is only one drive on the ribbon cable, and Cable Select. You can use a Cable Select configuration when you are using a Cable Select ribbon, which automatically designates one position on the cable as master and the other as slave. In general, for best performance, it is best to have drives on their own separate ribbon cable. If you need to install a second drive on a ribbon cable, choose the newest, fastest, or most used to act as Master. In this project, you will determine the hard-drive setup information for the drive to be installed, set the hard-drive jumpers, install the hard drive, and then configure the CMOS if the drive is not automatically detected. You can install the same hard drive as you removed in the previous project or a different one.
Outcomes	After completing this project, you will know how to: ▲ install an IDE hard drive
What you'll need	To complete this project, you will need: ▲ the computer from which you removed the hard drive in Project 7.2 ▲ a bootable floppy start-up disk ▲ an IDE hard drive compatible with the BIOS of the computer and the operating system that can be installed ▲ a ribbon cable for an IDE drive ▲ a Molex power connector that matches the plug on the drive ▲ a technician's tool kit with antistatic wrist strap and mat ▲ the manual that came with the drive (optional but recommended)
Completion time	60 minutes
Precautions	Be sure to take all necessary ESD precautions.

1. Research the settings for the new hard drive and record the jumper and CMOS setup information in the space provided:

   Jumper settings: _____

Cylinders: _____

Heads: _____

Sectors: _____

Note: Newer hard drives have diagrams of their jumper blocks on their labels.

2. If necessary, shut down the computer. Remove the power cable from the computer and carefully open the computer case. Locate an available drive bay, and identify where the cables will connect.

3. Set the jumpers on the new hard drive so they have the same function (master, slave, or cable select) as the drive you removed from the computer. The jumper blocks may be very different.

   Record how you set the jumpers. _____

4. Insert the new hard drive into the drive bay, securing it with mounting rails or screws.

5. Attach the ribbon cable (Figure 7-4) to the hard disk drive and motherboard or the hard disk controller, with the striped edge of the ribbon cable on pin 1 of the plugs. On early hard drives and on most new hard drives, the drive that is attached to the end of the ribbon cable is the **C:** drive. For some systems, the drive position on the ribbon cable does not matter.

Figure 7-4: Ribbon cable

6. Connect a power cable from the power supply to the drive.

7. Reassemble the computer (replace the expansion cards if you removed any and the cover).

8. Start the CMOS setup sequence and make sure the settings match those of the new drive. Usually the hard drive is automatically detected; however, if the computer BIOS does not automatically detect the drive, you must set the heads, cylinders, and sectors manually. Sometimes a hard drive is detected with the wrong settings. The wrong settings may cause the hard drive to be installed with the wrong size specified.

9. Exit the CMOS setup. The computer will reboot.

10. Boot to a startup disk in the **A:** drive and then type **A:\>C:** to attempt to access the hard drive you just installed.

11. If you see the message **INVALID DRIVE SPECIFICATION**, the drive needs to be formatted. Type **A:\>FORMAT C:** to format the new drive.

12. When the format is complete, type **A:\>C:** to access the hard drive.

13. If the **C:** prompt is displayed, the installation is a success.

Project 7.4	Installing a SATA Hard Drive
Overview	SATA drives are a faster alternative to IDE drives. They support greater storage capacities and higher data transfer speed. SATA drives use a narrower, and longer data cable that allows for better airflow and more flexibility in mounting a hard disk inside the PC case. The SATA power cable has a new type of 15-pin power connector. The SATA data cable connects to a new 7-pin IDE header directly integrated on the motherboard or on a PCI SATA expansion card. SATA drives also operate at lower voltages than IDE drives, reducing power consumption. Another important feature is that SATA drives are hot-swappable under Windows 2000, Windows XP, Windows Vista, and Windows Server 2003. One hard drive can be removed and another plugged in without rebooting the computer. The hot-swap feature and the higher data transfer speeds suggest that SATA drives may become a competitive alternative to SCSI hard disks. Many PC motherboards in current use do not have onboard support for SATA drives. SATA support can be added to these systems through PCI SATA expansion cards from third-party vendors. Typically, these expansion cards can support two or more SATA drives.
Outcomes	After completing this project, you will know how to: ▲ install a SATA hard drive in a computer
What you'll need	To complete this project, you will need: ▲ a Windows computer with a free drive bay and a motherboard that includes onboard SATA support (if it does not, you must first install a PCI SATA expansion card) ▲ an appropriate SATA hard drive ▲ a technician's toolkit with antistatic wrist strap
Completion time	60 minutes
Precautions	Be sure to take all necessary ESD precautions. You will need to ensure that drive you are installing is compatible with the motherboard.

1. Back up the data on existing hard disks in your PC.
2. Review the documentation included with your motherboard or third-party SATA expansion card. If necessary, install a PCI SATA expansion card if the motherboard does not include onboard SATA support.
3. Find an empty drive bay for the SATA drive; or rearrange the positions of existing storage devices, removing the old hard drive, if necessary.
4. Insert the SATA drive in the drive bay and secure it in place.

5. Attach the 4-pin side of a Molex-to-SATA power cable to a Molex cable from your power supply and attach the 15-pin side to the SATA power connector on the SATA drive (Figure 7-5). (A PC that includes direct SATA support may include a power supply with a native 15-pin power cable.)

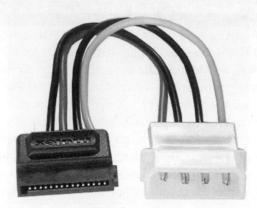

Figure 7-5: SATA power cable

6. Connect the 7-pin data cable to the SATA connector on the drive and to the SATA-1 header on the motherboard or PCI expansion card.

Figure 7-6: SATA data cable

7. Reconnect any drives, expansion cards, and internal cables that were disconnected duringthe drive installation. Reconnect the external video cable and power cable so that you can power on the computer and confirm that the system BIOS detects the drive properly. If the PC doesn't boot, the drive is either misconfigured or not detected at all. Remove and reattach cables as necessary.

Project 7.5	Installing a SCSI Host Adapter Card and Device Driver
Overview	SCSI (Small Computer Systems Interface) is an interface standard that supports a variety of internal and external peripheral devices, including hard drives. SCSI technology is typically found in server computers, but is also available for PCs Before you can install a SCSI hard drive into a computer system, the computer must be able to support it. Some computers have SCSI support built into their motherboards, or come with a SCSI adapter in a slot as standard equipment. If the computer does not have one of these two things, you must install a SCSI host adapter. A SCSI host adapter is used to manage all of the devices on the SCSI bus, as well as to send and retrieve data from the devices. There are a variety of host adapter cards available, including those compatible with 8-bit ISA, 16-bit ISA, and PCI buses. The host adapter chosen must be compatible with the motherboard's expansion buses. In this project you will learn how to install a SCSI host adapter card and confirm that its associated device driver has been installed.
Outcomes	After completing this project, you will know how to: ▲ install a SCSI host adapter card ▲ confirm that the SCSI host adapter device driver has been installed
What you'll need	To complete this project, you will need: ▲ a working computer that does not have a SCSI host adapter embedded on the motherboard ▲ an ISA, PCI, or PCI-X SCSI host adapter card/board (depending on the system's bus), and appropriate cables ▲ an available PCI or ISA slot ▲ a technician's toolkit with antistatic wrist strap ▲ documentation for the host adapter (recommended)
Completion time	60 minutes
Precautions	None

■ Part A: Install a SCSI host adapter

1. If necessary, shut down the computer and unplug it. Disconnect any external peripherals attached to the PC.
2. Carefully remove the computer case. **Note:** As soon as the cover is removed, use the antistatic wrist strap to protect the computer from ESD.
3. Locate an open expansion slot compatible with your host adapter.
4. If you are installing an older ISA host adapter card, you may need to configure jumpers or DIPswitches on the card before installing it. Check the manufacturer's documentation for any

required settings. Most modern host adapters (Figure 7-7) are Plug and Play, however, so this is likely to be unnecessary.

Figure 7-7: A typical host adapter card

5. Remove the slot cover from the back of the computer, and carefully insert the card into the available slot.

6. Secure the card in the slot with the case screw.

7. Reconnect the power cable and any other peripheral cables you disconnected.

8. Turn on the computer. As the computer starts, look at the monitor. Most SCSI host adapters display a start-up message with a prompt (a set of keystrokes) that allows you to enter the SCSI setup system. Note what you see.

_____

_____

_____

9. If there is an option to enter the SCSI setup system, type the prompt. In the SCSI setup, review and record the options offered. Refer to the host adapter card's manual for any details about the SCSI setup options.

_____

_____

■ **Part B**: **Confirm installation of the SCSI host adapter device driver**

1. Most host adapter cards today are Plug and Play. When you restart the computer, Windows should detect the presence of the adapter card and prompt you through the process of installing the host adapter's drive. Do so.

2. Once the driver is installed, use **Device Manager** to confirm that this software was properly installed. To open **Device Manager** in Windows XP, right-click **My Computer** in the **Start** menu, and select **Properties** on the shortcut menu to open the **Systems Properties** dialog box. Click the **Hardware** tab, and then click the Device Manager button to open the **Device Manager**. You should see an entry for your host adapter under **SCSI and RAID Controllers**.

Project 7.6	Replacing a SCSI Hard Drive
Overview	Unlike IDE devices, which usually have one jumper to select between master, slave, or cable select status, SCSI devices have three jumpers to set their ID number. These jumpers provide eight binary combinations from 000 to 111. The host adapter (SCSI controller) is usually device 7, whereas a bootable hard drive is usually device 0. Up to eight SCSI devices can be connected to the same SCSI-1 or SCSI narrow cable; the first and last devices on the cable are terminated with a resistor bank. The terminating resistor bank can be physically inserted or removed, it can be electrically inserted or removed by a single jumper, or it can be set with software. SCSI devices can be connected as internal devices, external devices, or a combination of internal and external devices. Internal SCSI devices usually use a 50-pin ribbon cable; there are several types of external SCSI cables. Consult the installation manual for cabling instructions.
	In this project, you will record the current hard-drive setup information, remove the hard drive, determine the hard-drive setup information for the drive to be installed, set the hard-drive jumpers, install the hard drive, and check the SCSI configuration to see if the hard drive is configured. You can install the same hard drive or a different one. Any hard drive you install must be compatible with the BIOS of your computer, the SCSI controller, and the operating system you are using.

Outcomes	After completing this project, you will know how to: ▲ remove a SCSI hard drive ▲ install a SCSI hard drive
What you'll need	To complete this project, you will need: ▲ a computer with a SCSI hard drive and host adapter installed ▲ a bootable floppy start-up disk ▲ a new internal SCSI hard drive to install (alternatively, you can reinstall the SCSI hard drive that you removed in Part A of the project) ▲ a power connector inside the computer that matches the plug on the new drive (usually a Molex) ▲ an internal terminator, if the host adapter doesn't already have one built in ▲ an interface cable (usually a ribbon cable) with the appropriate connectors for connecting the new drive to the host adapter ▲ a technician's toolkit with antistatic wrist strap and antistatic mat
Completion time	60 minutes
Precautions	Be sure to take all necessary ESD precautions. Also make sure that any data on the hard drive that you will be removing has been backed up.

■ Part A: Remove the current SCSI hard drive

1. If necessary, turn on the computer, and access the CMOS setup routine (also referred to as the BIOS setup program or BIOS screen). The CMOS setup routine is available for only a short time during the book sequence. Most computer manufacturers tell you how to enter the CMOS startup screen as the computer is booting, typically by pressing a specific key combination, such as F2 or Ctrl +F1. The initial screen typically displays a menu of configuration categories, each of which lead to one or more additional menu screens and options. Select the **Drive Configuration** option and press the Enter key. Record the information that appears.

   _____

   _____

   _____

2. When you have finished recording the information, press the Escape key and allow the computer to finish booting.

3. Shut down the computer and unplug it. Disconnect any external peripheral cables.

4. Carefully remove the computer case cover. **Note:** After you remove the cover, use the antistatic wrist strap to protect the computer from ESD.

5. Prepare a sketch that shows where each expansion card goes in the motherboard expansion slots and where any cables or wires are connected to the expansion card. On this sketch, note the pin 1 edge (the edge that has a stripe) on the cables and the colors of individual wires attached to the expansion card.

---

6. If any of the expansion cards are obstructing your access to the hard drive, you will need to remove them. Disconnect the wires and cables that are connected to the expansion card, remove the mounting screw, grasp the expansion card with both hands, and pull upward while gently rocking the board from front to back. **Note:** As soon as the expansion card is out, place it on an antistatic mat to protect against ESD.

7. The power cable plug on the hard drive is keyed so it fits only one way, but the ribbon (data) cable can be accidentally reversed if it is not keyed. To keep this from happening, note the pin 1 position of the hard drive so you can later match it with the striped edge on the data cable when the drive is reinstalled. After you've done this, disconnect the data cable (ribbon cable) and power cable from the hard drive.

8. Physically remove the hard drive from the computer. Unbolt the hard drive from the drive bay and then remove the drive from the computer.

9. In another sketch, draw the hard-drive jumper block and show the current jumper settings and terminating resistor. The jumper settings should be a binary number from 000 to 111. The boot hard drive is usually set to binary 0, which is indicated by no SCSI ID jumpers being set. The first and last devices on the cable are terminated with a resistor bank.

■ Part B: Install a SCSI drive

1. Verify the hard-drive CMOS settings. The CMOS should be set to SCSI or NO DRIVE. Record the information.

   _____

   Note: Newer hard drives have diagrams of their jumper blocks on their labels.

2. Set the jumpers on the new hard drive to have the same SCSI ID number as the drive you removed from the computer. Set the terminating resistor if it was set on the hard drive you removed.

   Record how you set the jumpers: _____

3. Place the new hard drive in the drive bay and secure it with screws or mounting rails or screws.

4. Attach the SCSI ribbon cable to the hard disk drive and the SCSI host adapter, with the striped edge of the ribbon cable on pin 1 of the plugs (Figure 7-8).

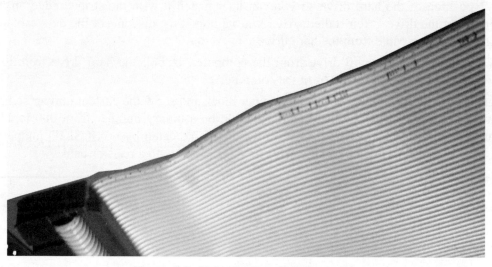

Figure 7-8: Striped edge of ribbon cable

5. Attach a power cable to from the power supply the drive.

6. Reassemble the computer (replace the expansion cards if you removed any and the cover).

7. Boot the computer and press Ctrl + A. You should see the message **Press Ctrl+A for SCSI Select**. The SCSI hard drive should appear in the SCSI scan.

8. Boot to a startup disk in drive A: and then attempt to access the hard drive you just installed by typing **A:\>C:**

9. If you see the message **INVALID DRIVE SPECIFICATION**, the drive needs to be formatted. Type **A:\>FORMAT C:** to format the new drive.

10. When the format is complete, type **A:\>C:** to access the hard drive.
11. If the computer shows a **C:** prompt, the installation was a success.

Project 7.7	Partitioning and Formatting a Hard Disk Drive
Overview	For a hard disk to be able to hold files and programs, it has to be partitioned and formatted. Partitioning is the process of creating logical divisions on a hard drive. A hard drive can have one or more partitions, represented by different drive letters. Formatting is the process of preparing a hard disk for use by an operating system. Formatting establishes a file system, creates and configures a file allocation table (FAT), and creates a root directory. Different operating systems support different types of file systems, such as FAT16, FAT32, and NTFS. In this project, you will learn how to partition unallocated space on a hard disk and format it.
Outcomes	After completing this project, you will know how to: ▲ partition a hard disk ▲ format a hard disk
What you'll need	To complete this project, you will need: ▲ administrative rights on a Windows XP, Windows 2000 or Windows Server 2003 computer that has an additional unpartitioned hard drive installed. You can also use a computer whose hard disk is set up to use basic storage and has unallocated space available
Completion time	30 minutes
Precautions	Do not tamper with the logical drive (usually the C: drive) that contains the Windows system files.

1. If necessary, turn on the computer and log on as an Administrator.
2. Open the **Start** menu, select **Control Panel**, and then select **Administrative Tools** to open the **Computer Management** window.
3. Double-click **Storage** in the left pane of the window if necessary, and then click **Disk Management** to display the disk configuration information in the **Details** pane.
4. Record the information about the hard disks and other storage devices that you see.

_____

_____

_____

5. Right-click an area of unpartitioned space, and choose **New Partition** on the shortcut menu.

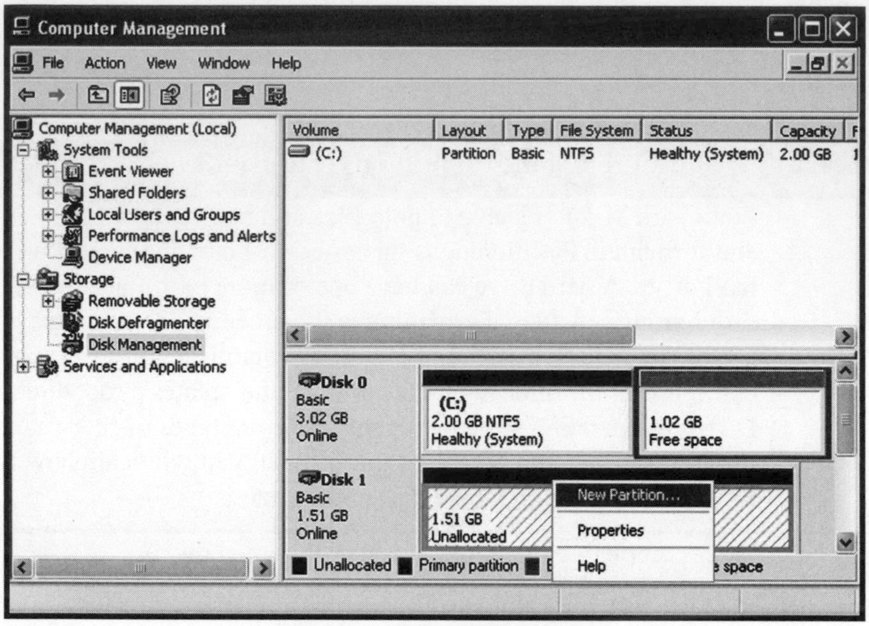

Figure 7-9: Disk Management

6. The **Welcome** screen of the **New Partition Wizard** appears, with information on creating a partition. Click the Next button to continue.

7. The **Select Partition Type** screen appears. You have the option of selecting either a primary partition or an extended partition. The **Primary Partition** option button should be selected by default.

8. Record the information available on this screen about how many primary partitions can be created on a basic disk.

_____

_____

9. Accept the default selection (**Primary Partition**) by clicking the Next button.

10. The **Specify Partition** screen appears. Here, you must select the size for the partition. (**Note:** Choose a partition size that is no greater than one-half of the size of the unallocated space.) Enter a value for the size of the partition in the **Amount of disk space to be used** spin box. Record the maximum disk space, the minimum disk space, and the size that you selected.

_____

_____

_____

11. Click the Next button to open the **Assign Drive Letter or Path** screen. Here, you can assign a drive letter or path for the partition. (**Note:** You can always change the drive letter and path at a later date.) Typically, the computer's initial hard drive will be assigned the letter C, with D: assigned to a CD-ROM or DVD-ROM drive. Here, accept the default assignment.

12. Click the Next button to open the **Format Partition** screen. Here, a file system for the drive must be selected. NTFS is the file system selected by default. What are the other file systems available?

_____

_____

_____

13. Choose **NTFS** as the file system, and enter a label (name) for the partition in the **Volume label** text box. Record the label that you selected.

_____

14. Make sure the **Perform a Quick Format** checkbox is selected.

15. Click the Next button.

16. The **Completing the New Partition Wizard** screen appears. Review the information presented, and then click the **Finish** button to complete the process.

17. Return to the **Computer Management** window to see the newly created primary partition.

18. Close the **Computer Management** window, and all other open windows.

19. What are some other methods available to partition and format a hard disk drive?

_____

_____

_____

_____

Project 7.8	Defragmenting a Hard Drive
Overview	When you create a file, it normally occupies contiguous hard-drive space (the clusters used to store the file are adjacent to each other). Over time, as the file size increases, there may not be enough contiguous space for the file. So, the file gets broken up. This process is called *fragmentation*. When enough files become fragmented, the hard drive wastes time going to different clusters to retrieve them. If fragmentation becomes bad enough, a condition called *disk thrashing* occurs: Operations slow noticeably, and the hard-drive light flickers to indicate constant activity. Microsoft provides a utility called Disk Defragmenter to help the hard drive reorganize itself. Defragmentation is a process of rewriting files and organizing them so that access to the files is improved. This process can take several hours if you do not have adequate free space for the system to rewrite files or if there is a lot of fragmentation on the hard drive. In this project you will learn how to use the Disk Defragmenter to analyze the level of fragmentation of a hard drive, and defragment it if necessary.
Outcomes	After completing this project, you will know how to: ▲ analyze a hard disk to determine its level of fragmentation ▲ defragment a hard drive
What you'll need	To complete this project, you will need: ▲ administrative rights on a Windows XP, Windows 2000 or Windows Server 2003 computer
Completion time	30 minutes or more depending on the amount of fragmentation
Precautions	Run Disk Defragmenter only when you are not using the computer for anything else. The defragmentation process can slow the time it takes to access other disk-based resources, and any files that are open or in use cannot be defragmented.

1. Turn on the computer, and log on as an administrator.
2. Open the **Start** menu and select **My Computer**.
3. Right-click the **C:** drive and click **Properties** to open the **Properties** dialog box
4. Click the **Tools** tab.

5. Click the Defragment Now button to open the **Disk Defragmenter** window (Figure 7-10).

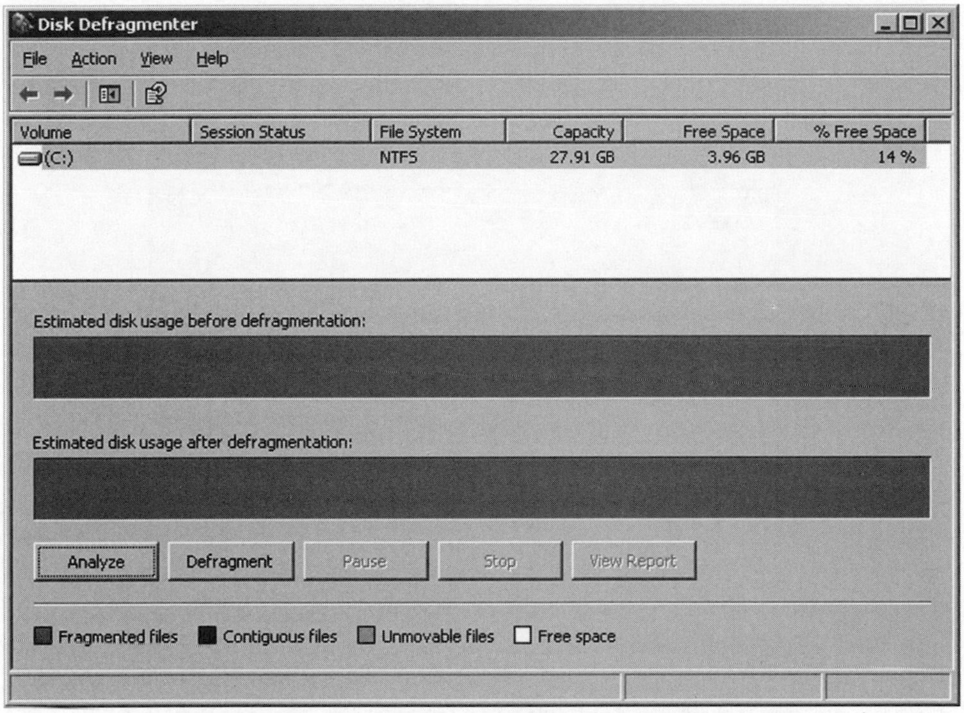

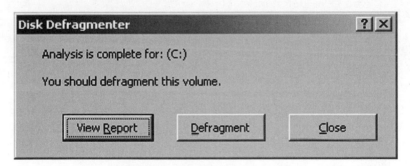

Figure 7-10: Disk Defragmenter window

6. Click the Analyze button.
7. The computer will now analyze the fragmentation of the hard disk drive. A message box will appear when the analysis is complete, with a recommendation as to whether the volume should be defragmented (Figure 7-11).

Figure 7-11: Analysis completed

8. Click the View Report button. An **Analysis Report** dialog box opens (Figure 7-12).

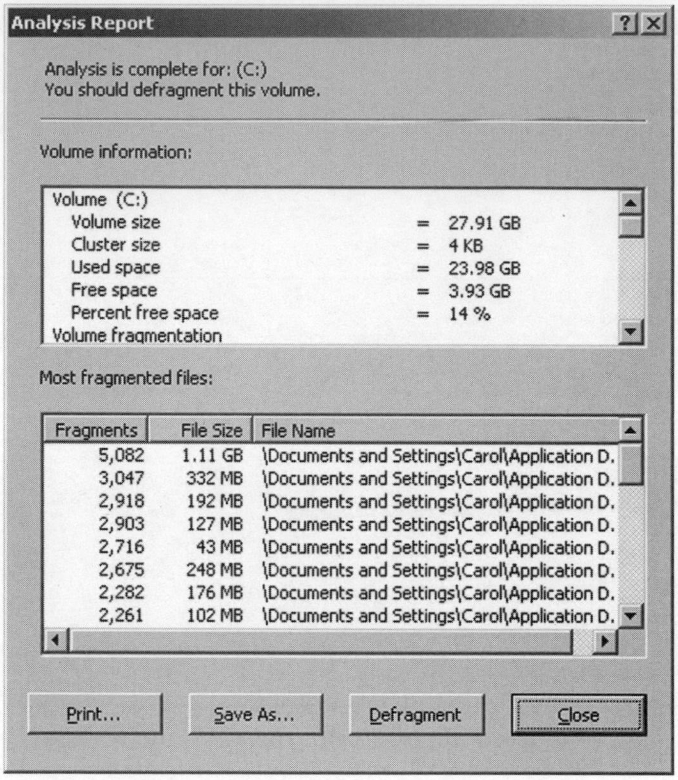

Figure 7-12: Analysis Report dialog box

9. Record the following volume information:

Volume size: _____

Cluster size:_____

Used space:_____

Free space:_____

Percent free space: _____

10. Record the following information about the most fragmented file:

Fragments: _____

File size: _____

File name:_____

11. If defragmenting is recommended, click the Defragment button to start the defragmenting process. You can follow the process in the **Disk Defragmenter** window.

12. When the process is complete, a message box will appear. Click the Close button to close the message box.

13. Close the **Disk Defragmenter** and any other open windows.

8
REMOVABLE STORAGE

PROJECTS

Project 8.1	Removing a Floppy Drive
Overview	The floppy drive has become increasingly unnecessary due to the advent of optical compact disk technology as the primary method of removable storage. However, floppy drives are still useful for storing and transferring small data files. For this reason, you should know how to remove and replace floppy drives. In this project, you will practice removing a floppy drive from a computer.
Outcomes	After completing this project, you will know how to: ▲ remove a floppy drive from a computer
What you'll need	To complete this project, you will need: ▲ a computer equipped with a 3.5" floppy disk drive ▲ a technician's toolkit and antistatic wrist strap
Completion time	30 minutes
Precautions	As always, take the necessary precautions to guard against ESD when opening up the computer. Also, replacing a floppy disk drive in any computer means you may lose the computer's CMOS disk drive settings. Without its CMOS data, the computer won't work, so you must be able to replace this data. Therefore, you should make a record of this data before you begin the process of floppy-drive replacement.

1. Run the CMOS setup routine and record the following drive data below:

    Drive A Physical Size: _____

    Drive A Capacity: _____

    Drive B Physical Size: _____

    Drive B Capacity: _____

    Drive C Cylinders: _____

    Drive C Heads: _____

    Drive C Sectors: _____

    Drive D Cylinders: _____

    Drive D Heads: _____

Drive D Sectors: _____

2. Boot the computer, place a floppy disk in the **A:** drive, right-click the **A:** drive icon in the **My Computer** window, and then click **Explore** to display the floppy disk's contents to verify that the **A:** drive is operational.

3. Shut down the computer and turn off the power to all peripherals attached to the computer.

4. Open the computer case.

5. As soon as the cover is removed, put on your antistatic wrist strap to protect the computer from ESD.

6. If any of the expansion cards are obstructing your access to the floppy drive, you need to remove them. But before doing so, prepare a sketch that shows where each expansion card goes in the motherboard expansion slots and where any cables or wires are connected to the expansion card. On your sketch, note the pin 1 edge (the edge that has a stripe) on the cables and the colors of individual wires attached to the expansion card. Room for your sketch has been provided below.

7. Once you complete your sketch, disconnect any wires and cables connected to the expansion cards that are obstructing your access and remove the cards one at a time. To remove a card, remove the mounting screw, grasp the expansion card with both hands, and pull upward while gently rocking the board from front to back (refer back to Project 7.2).

8. As soon as the expansion card is out, place it on an antistatic mat to protect against ESD. Any expansion cards that are removed must be reinstalled before you replace the computer cover.

9. The power cable plug on the floppy drive is keyed so it fits only one way, but the ribbon (data) cable can be accidentally reversed. To keep this from happening, note the pin 1 position of the floppy drive so you can later match it with the striped edge on the data cable when the drive is reinstalled. After you've done this, disconnect the ribbon (data) cable and power cable from the floppy drive. Note the pin 1 position to the controller on the motherboard and remove the floppy cable from the controller.

10. To remove the floppy drive from the computer, unbolt or release the floppy drive from the drive bay and pull the drive out of the front of the computer. You may have to remove the front panel to do this.

Project 8.2	Installing a Floppy Drive
Overview	Installing a floppy drive is a straightforward process, but as with any exercise in which the computer cover is removed, you should still use caution during the installation. In this exercise, you will use the drive that you removed in Project 8.1 (or a new floppy drive, if you have one available) to practice installing floppy drives quickly and easily.
Outcomes	After completing this project, you will know how to: ▲ install a floppy drive in a computer
What you'll need	To complete this project, you will need: ▲ a computer without a floppy drive whose motherboard has a floppy connector ▲ an appropriate floppy drive to install (you can also reinstall the floppy drive removed in Project 8.1) ▲ a technician's toolkit with antistatic wrist strap
Completion time	30 minutes
Precautions	As always, take the necessary precautions to guard against ESD when opening up the computer.

1. Slide the drive (Figure 8-1) into the drive bay and fasten it in.

Figure 8-1: A floppy drive

2. Attach the DC power connector to the drive.
3. Attach the ribbon (data) cable to the drive, with the striped edge of the ribbon cable on pin 1 of the floppy-drive plug. If this is the only floppy drive in the computer, it is drive **A:** and must be attached to a connector that is between the twisted wires and the end of the cable. If this is a second floppy drive, it is drive **B:**. Drive **B:** must be attached between the twist in the floppy-drive cable and the floppy-drive controller.

4. Attach the ribbon cable to the controller with the striped edge on the cable connected to pin 1 on the controller (Figure 8-2).

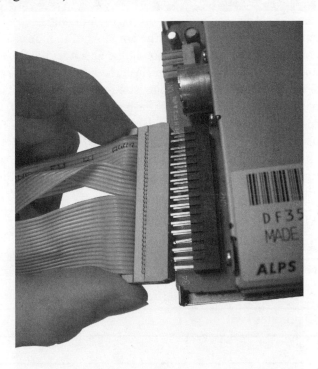

Figure 8-2: Attaching the ribbon cable to a drive

5. Using the sketch you made, reinstall all expansion cards that you removed. To install an expansion card, place the card in the same motherboard slot from which you removed it and press down firmly until the card is seated in the slot. Reconnect any cables or wires you disconnected from the card, and then replace the expansion card screw.

6. Replace the computer cover and connect all external cables.

7. Run the CMOS setup sequence. If the floppy drive indicated in the CMOS is incorrect for the new drive, select the type of drive you installed. When you exit CMOS setup, the computer will reboot, and the new settings will be loaded.

8. Boot the computer, place a floppy disk in the **A:** drive, right-click the **A:** drive icon in the **My Computer** window, and then click **Explore** to display the floppy disk's contents to verify that the **A:** drive is operational.

9. If the **A:** drive isn't working, check whether the floppy-drive light is always on. A floppy-drive light that is constantly on usually indicates that the data cable is upside down.

Project 8.3	Working with Flash Memory
Overview	Flash memory has rapidly become a viable alternative to disk memory for data storage. It can store large amounts of memory on a single chip, and continues to store information in the absence of a power source. There are a number of different types of flash memory devices, including memory cards (Figure 8-3) that are used data storage in digital cameras and other mobile or handheld devices, and USB flash drives (Figure 8-4), which are designed for removable storage for a PC. However, flash memory sacrifices cost for its improved storage capacity, as it is a fairly expensive way to store data, although prices have been dropping rapidly. In this exercise, you will familiarize yourself with flash memory and learn to distinguish between its different types.
Outcomes	After completing this project, you will know how to: ▲ differentiate between types of flash memory
What you'll need	To complete this project, you will need: ▲ a computer with Internet access
Completion time	30 minutes
Precautions	None

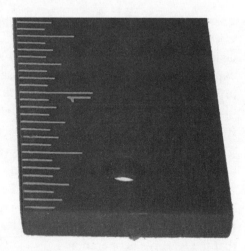

Figure 8-3: Flash memory card

Figure 8-4: USB flash drive

1. What are three main kinds of flash memory?

    _____

    _____

    _____

2. List at least three devices where flash memory is used.

    _____

    _____

    _____

3. Do an Internet search for 'flash memory' and find an online retailer with a good selection of flash memory. Find three memory cards and record their memory size, write speed, and price below.

    Card 1

    Memory: _____

    Dimensions: _____

    Price: _____

    Card 2

    Memory: _____

    Dimensions: _____

    Price: _____

Card 3

Memory: _____

Dimensions: _____

Price: _____

3. Which of the three cards would you use if you had to maximize storage space and why? Which would you use if you wanted a low-cost device to store small files and why? Which would you use if you required a card for a 24mm x 32 mm slot and why?

_____

_____

_____

4. Search the same online retailer for USB flash drives. What are the most common flash drive sizes? What is the largest size drive available?

_____

_____

_____

5. What is the limit to the number of times a flash drive can be used?

_____

6. Describe the steps you would take to determine whether a computer can be booted from a USB flash drive.

_____

_____

_____

_____

7. What procedure should you follow to safely remove a USB flash drive?

_____

_____

_____

Project 8.4	Installing a CD/DVD Drive
Overview	Optical drives have replaced floppy drives as the most common method for removable storage. This is because of their much greater data storage capabilities. A floppy disk holds 1.44 MB of data, whereas an optical disk holds upwards of 650 MB. Adding a CD or DVD drive is a common upgrade, so you will need to be familiar with how to install them. CD-RW, CD-R, DVD-ROM, and any other removable media drives that use CD-ROM technology can be installed using these same steps.
Outcomes	After completing this project, you will know how to: ▲ install a CD/DVD drive in a computer
What you'll need	To complete this project, you will need: ▲ a Windows computer with a free 5 ¼" drive bay ▲ an appropriate CD or DVD drive ▲ a technician's toolkit with antistatic wrist strap
Completion time	60 minutes
Precautions	Be sure to have ESD materials available. You will need to ensure that drive you are installing is compatible with the motherboard.

■ Part A: Install a CD-ROM drive in a one IDE port system

1. Set the hard-drive jumpers to the cable select position. The jumper positions are usually documented on the drive. If you are not installing a new hard drive or CD-ROM, you will need to remove them first.
2. Set the CD-ROM drive jumpers (Figure 8-5) to the slave position. The jumper positions are usually documented on the drive.

Figure 8-5: ATA CD-ROM drive jumpers and audio connectors

3.   Mount the CD-ROM drive in the empty drive bay (Figure 8-6).

Figure 8-6: Empty drive bay

4.   Connect the second port on the hard-drive IDE cable to the CD-ROM drive. Be sure to connect the striped edge of the ribbon cable to pin 1 of the CD-ROM drive.

5.   Connect the power cable to the CD-ROM drive.

6.   Boot the computer to the **Desktop** and look for the CD-ROM drive in the **My Computer** window.

7.   If the CD-ROM icon does not appear in **My Computer**, open the **Control Panel** and click **Add New Hardware** and follow the Wizard's instructions.

8.   If the CD-ROM icon still does not appear in **My Computer**, go back to step 1.

9.   For Windows versions earlier than Windows XP, you will probably be asked to insert a device driver disk to enable features other than reading a CD.

■ Part B: Install a CD-ROM drive in a system with two IDE ports

1.   Obtain an IDE ribbon cable and connect it to the second IDE port. Do not disturb the first IDE port or the hard drive(s) attached to it. Be sure to connect the striped edge of the ribbon cable to pin 1 of the IDE port.

2.   Set the CD-ROM drive jumpers to the master position.

3. Mount the CD-ROM drive in the drive bay.

4. Connect the second IDE port cable to the CD-ROM drive. Be sure to connect the striped edge of the ribbon cable to pin 1 of the CD-ROM drive.

5. Connect the power cable to the CD-ROM drive.

6. Boot the computer and look for the CD-ROM drive in the **My Computer** window.

7. If the CD-ROM icon does not appear in **My Computer**, open the **Control Panel** and click **Add New Hardware** and follow the Wizard's instructions.

8. If the CD-ROM icon still does not appear in My Computer, go back to Step 1.

9. For Windows versions earlier than Windows XP, you will probably be asked to insert the device driver disk to enable features other than reading a CD.

Project 8.5	Researching Media Types
Overview	The many different kinds of CD and DVD formats can be overwhelming for the casual computer user. In this project, you will familiarize yourself with these formats and learn what distinguishes them from one another. Use the Internet to obtain the information needed to answer these questions.
Outcomes	After completing this project, you will know how to: ▲ differentiate between different CD and DVD formats
What you'll need	To complete this project, you will need: ▲ a computer with Internet access
Completion time	60 minutes
Precautions	None

1. What is the primary difference between the CD-R and CD-RW format?

    _____

    _____

    _____

2. What are some differences between the CD-R and DVD-R format?

    _____

    _____

    _____

3. Approximately how many times may a DVD-RW be rewritten?

    _____

4. What are some advantages of the DVD+RW format compared to DVD-RW?

    _____

    _____

    _____

5. What are some disadvantages of the DVD+RW format compared to DVD-RW?

    _____

    _____

    _____

6. List three properties of the DVD-RAM format.

    _____

    _____

    _____

Project 8.6	Comparing CD/DVD Drive Types
Overview	Removable storage can accomplish a wide variety of tasks. However, there are many different kinds of drives, each of which have unique characteristics. In this project, you will use the Internet to help you learn to differentiate between the many types of removable storage and to choose appropriate types in different scenarios. You will be working only with CD/DVD drives in this project.
Outcomes	After completing this project, you will know how to: ▲ identify and purchase the appropriate CD/DVD drive
What you'll need	To complete this project, you will need: ▲ a computer with Internet access
Completion time	60 minutes
Precautions	None

1. Perform a web search for 'removable storage' or 'CD/DVD drives'. Find an online retailer with a good selection of drives. If you can't find one, try Tiger Direct or CDW.

2. Pick three CD/DVD drives and record the following information about them:

Drive 1

Name: _____

Supported media types: _____

CD Write Speed (if applicable): _____

CD Rewrite Speed (if applicable): _____

DVD-R Write Speed (if applicable): _____

DVD+R Write Speed (if applicable): _____

Price: _____

Drive 2

Name: _____

Supported media types: _____

CD Write Speed (if applicable): _____

CD Rewrite Speed (if applicable): _____

DVD-R Write Speed (if applicable): _____

DVD+R Write Speed (if applicable): _____

Price: _____

Drive 3

Name: _____

Supported media types: _____

CD Write Speed (if applicable): _____

CD Rewrite Speed (if applicable): _____

DVD-R Write Speed (if applicable): _____

DVD+R Write Speed (if applicable): _____

Price: _____

4. Assume that you are a casual computer user looking to upgrade your CD/DVD drive. You would like to get a drive with CD-RW capability, but you do not expect to require anything more advanced than that. You want to minimize the price of your new drive as much as you can. Which of your three choices would be most appropriate and why?

_____

_____

_____

5. Assume that you are a computer enthusiast looking to upgrade your CD/DVD drive to an advanced model. It must be compatible with as many media types as possible, since you want to be prepared to work with any format. You are willing to sacrifice price and speed for functionality. Which of your three choices would be most appropriate and why?

_____

_____

_____

6. Assume that you are the sales manager for a small business. You need a drive that you can use to quickly create copies of your new product to send to potential customers. You are looking for a drive with fast write speeds. The media types that it must be compatible with are CD-RW and DVD-R. Which of your three choices would be most appropriate and why?

_____

_____

_____

9

INPUT AND OUTPUT DEVICES

PROJECTS

Project 9.1	Working with the Mouse
Overview	A mouse is one of the most important I/O devices for a desktop computer. In this project, you will practice maintaining a mechanical mouse as well as installing a mouse on your computer. If you have a trackball or an optical mouse, you can still perform the installation portion of the project, but the steps for preventive maintenance will not apply.
Outcomes	After completing this project, you will know how to: ▲ perform preventive maintenance on a mechanical mouse ▲ install a mouse on your computer ▲ configure a mouse ▲ troubleshoot mouse problems
What you'll need	To complete this project, you will need: ▲ a mechanical mouse and a Windows XP computer to which you can attach it
Completion time	30 minutes
Precautions	None

■ Part A: Perform preventive maintenance on a mouse

1. Open the ball access cover. You usually do this by either rotating or sliding the locking collar that holds the mouse ball in place. Usually, large arrows show the direction you must push or twist.

2. Clean the ball with a swab and a mild soap. Don't rub the mouse with a pencil eraser to clean it. And don't use anything that could react with the rubber to cause flat spots or make the mouse ball less round, such as contact cleaner or alcohol.

3. Often the problem with a dirty mouse is that the rollers deep inside the mouse have become dirty or clogged with lint. First use tweezers to remove any lint on the rollers. Then use the same cleaner you used for the ball to clean the rollers with a clean swab.

4. Blow compressed air into the ball housing. Replace the ball and reinstall the retaining ring. Test the mouse immediately and correct any problems that appear.

■ Part B: Install a mouse

1. If either the current mouse or the mouse you are installing is not a USB mouse, turn the computer off.
2. Unplug the old mouse.
3. Plug the new mouse into the appropriate port on the computer (Figure 9-1).

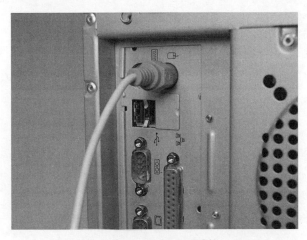

Figure 9-1: Connecting a PS/2 mouse

4. Turn your computer on if you had to turn it off.
5. Windows can detect almost all mice and enable them to function. However, any special functions that your mouse has may need to be enabled by software, which you can now install through the manufacturer's CD-ROM disks.

■ Part C: Configure mouse properties

1. Open the **Start** menu and select **Control Panel** to open the **Control Panel** window. Switch to **Classic View**, if necessary (all of the projects in this chapter assume Windows XP is in **Classic View**).

2. Double-click the **Mouse** icon to open the **Mouse Properties** dialog box (Figure 9-2).

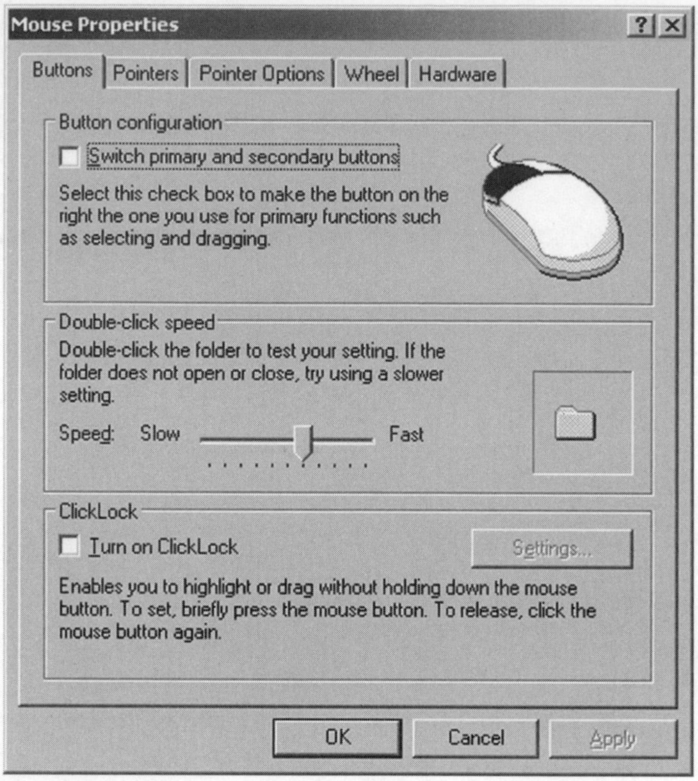

Figure 9-2: The Mouse Properties dialog box

3. What mouse settings can you configure via the **Mouse Properties** dialog box?

_____

_____

4. On the **Buttons** tab, in the **Button configuration** section, select the **Switch primary and secondary buttons** check box. Then use your mouse. What happens?

_____

_____

5. Click the **Hardware** tab, and record the information you find there.

_____

_____

6. Click the Properties button on the **Hardware** tab. The **Properties** dialog box for the mouse appears.

7. Select the **Driver** tab. Click the Driver Details button. Record the information you find there.

_____

_____

8. Is the driver signed? _____

9. What mouse driver maintenance activities can you perform via the **Driver** tab?

_____

_____

_____

■ **Part D: Troubleshoot mouse problems**

1. Open the **Mouse Properties** dialog box to the **Hardware** tab.

2. Click the Troubleshoot button to open the **Mouse Troubleshooter** page in the **Windows XP Help and Support Center**.

3. What information about troubleshooting mouse problems does Microsoft provide?

_____

_____

_____

Project 9.2	Working with the Keyboard
Overview	Keyboards enable computer users to communicate with the computer by using keystrokes. Along with the mouse, they are among the most commonly used I/O devices for any computer. In this project, you will practice cleaning a keyboard as well as installing one, configuring keyboard properties, examining the driver for the keyboard and troubleshooting keyboard problems.
Outcomes	After completing this project, you will know how to: ▲ perform preventive maintenance on a keyboard ▲ install a keyboard ▲ configure keyboard properties ▲ troubleshoot keyboard problems

What you'll need	To complete this project, you will need:
	▲ a functional keyboard and a Windows XP computer to which you can attach it
Completion time	30 minutes
Precautions	None

■ Part A: Perform preventive maintenance on a keyboard

1. Turn the keyboard upside down and shake out any debris.
2. Use compressed air to dislodge any remaining debris. You can buy cans of compressed air on the web or at many computer retail stores.
3. Spray some all-purpose cleaner onto a soft cloth and wipe key tops with the dampened cloth.
4. Use a lint-free swab dampened with the cleaner to clean between the keys.

■ Part B: Install a keyboard

1. If your current or new keyboard is not a USB keyboard, shut down your computer.
2. Disconnect the current keyboard.
3. Connect the cable of the new keyboard into the appropriate port on the computer (Figure 9-3).

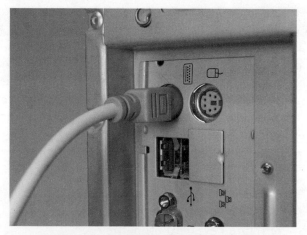

Figure 9-3: Connecting a PS/2 keyboard

4. Turn your computer back on if you had to turn it off.

5. Windows should automatically detect and enable most keyboards. If your keyboard has any special functionality, however, you will now need to install any manufacturer software that came on a CD-ROM disk with the keyboard.

■ Part C: Configure keyboard properties

1. Open the **Control Panel**, and double-click the **Keyboard** icon to open the **Keyboard Properties** dialog box (Figure 9-4).

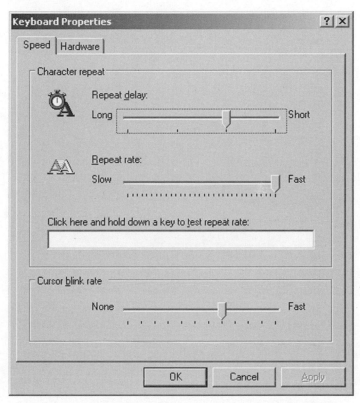

Figure 9-4: The Keyboard Properties dialog box

2. Examine the **Speed** tab.

3. What is the function of the repeat delay?

_____

4. What is the repeat delay set at?

_____

5. What is the function of the Repeat rate?

_____

6. What is the repeat rate set at?

_____

7. Change the rates, then click in the test box near the middle of the dialog box to test your new settings.

8. Click the **Hardware** tab (Figure 9-5).

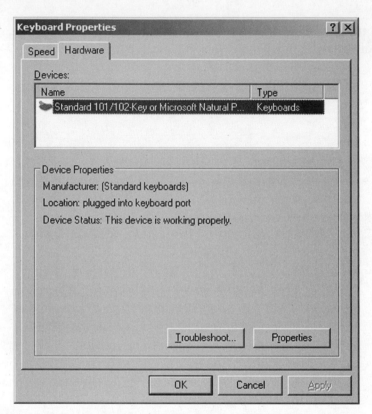

Figure 9-5: The Hardware tab in the Keyboard Properties dialog box

9. Record the information you see there.

_____

_____

_____

■ Part D: Examine the driver for the keyboard

1. Open the **Keyboard Properties** dialog box to the **Hardware** tab.
2. Click the Properties button. The **Properties** dialog box for the keyboard appears.
3. Select the **Driver** tab. Click the Driver Details button. Record the information you find there.

_____

_____

4. Is the driver signed?

_____

Part E: Troubleshoot keyboard problems

1. Open the **Keyboard Properties** dialog box to the **Hardware** tab.
2. Click the Troubleshoot button to open the **Keyboard Troubleshooter** page in the **Windows XP Help and Support Center**.
3. What information about troubleshooting keyboard problems does Microsoft provide?

_____

_____

_____

_____

Project 9.3	Working with the Monitor
Overview	Monitors are the most prominent form of display technologies. Anyone who has used a computer knows how essential a monitor is to its function. In this project, you will perform maintenance on a monitor and install a CRT monitor to your computer.
	Once your monitor is installed, you can modify its display settings, such as the screen resolution, color quality, and background colors. Resolution affects the image quality that appears on the monitor. In this project, you will practice configuring display resolution and other display settings. To configure display settings on a Windows XP computer, you use the Settings tab in the Display Properties dialog box.
	The Settings tab, you can access the Troubleshoot button, which you can use to solve problems related to a monitor's display settings. The Troubleshoot button opens the Video Display Troubleshooter in the Windows XP Help and Support Center.
Outcomes	After completing this project, you will know how to:
	▲ perform preventive maintenance on a monitor
	▲ install a monitor
	▲ configure display properties
	▲ troubleshoot display problems
What you'll need	To complete this project, you will need:
	▲ a working monitor and a Windows XP computer to which you can attach it
Completion time	30 minutes
Precautions	**Do not open a monitor to work on it**. The monitor holds at least 20,000 volts, even with the power off. If you open a monitor, you run the risk of coming into contact with potentially lethal voltages.
	Check with your instructor to make sure that the monitor's display controls have not bee locked. If they have, skip Step 4 of Part B.

■ Part A: Perform preventive maintenance on a CRT or LCD monitor

1. First, power off the monitor. If clean a monitor while it is powered, you may be a conduit for the static electricity built up on the screen.
2. Use a lint-free cloth dampened with water to gently wipe the glass of a CRT monitor or the screen of an LCD monitor. For an LCD screen, avoid abrasive cleaners and pads. You can use a mild detergent or general purpose cleaner with a soft cloth.

■ Part B: Install a CRT monitor

1. Attach the monitor's system cable to the appropriate monitor port on the back of the computer. Don't force the cable if it doesn't connect smoothly.

2. Make sure that that the cable is connected securely, and screw in the retaining screws to the sockets on the port.

3. Plug the monitor's power cable into a wall outlet and test the power. If the power light on the monitor turns on, you have plugged in the cable correctly.

4. Use the monitor's display controls to optimize the display quality of your monitor. You may need to refer to the manufacturer's manual for more information on changing the display quality. Adjust the brightness, contrast, and other options so that the display is to your liking.

■ Part C: Set display properties

1. To open the **Display Properties** dialog box, right-click an empty space on the Windows desktop and select **Properties** from the shortcut menu.

2. Explore the tabs in the **Display Properties** dialog box. What do the **Themes**, **Desktop**, **Screen Saver**, and **Appearance** tabs allow you to do?

Themes:

_____

_____

Desktop:

_____

_____

Screen Saver:

_____

_____

Appearance:

_____

_____

3. Select the **Settings** tab (Figure 9-6).

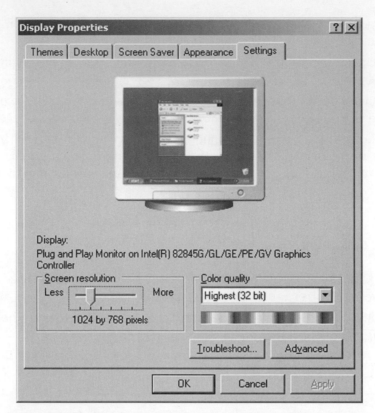

Figure 9-6: The Settings tab in the Display Properties dialog box

4. What is the screen resolution currently set at?

_____

5. Move the slide selector from side to side to adjust the size of the screen resolution to a new setting. Record the setting.

_____

6. What is the current color quality?

_____

7. From the drop-down list of colors, choose a different color setting. Record your choice.

_____

8. Click Apply to change the settings for your monitor. A **Monitor Settings** message box may appears, telling you that the desktop has been reconfigured and asks you if you want to keep the new settings. If so, you have 15 seconds in which to respond affirmatively; otherwise the display reverts to its previous setting.

9. Click Yes to proceed, then OK to close the **Display Properties** dialog box.

10. If you increase the resolution on your display, the images become smaller; if you decrease the resolution, they become larger.

11. Change the settings in the opposite direction to demonstrate the resolution range of your system.

12. Reset the settings back to your original settings, or if you found a new setting to your liking, keep it.

13. Click the Advanced button on the **Settings** tab. The **Properties** dialog box for the graphics controller card opens (Figure 9-7).

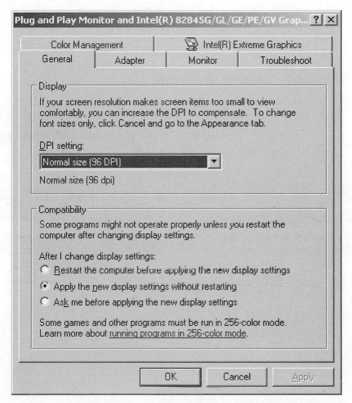

Figure 9-7: The Properties dialog box for the graphics controller card

14. Select the **Adapter** tab. Record the information about the adapter.

_____

_____

15. Select the **Monitor** tab. What kind of monitor is this?

_____

_____

16. What is the current refresh rate? What other refresh rates are supported by this monitor? What does increasing the refresh rate do?

_____

_____

17. Select the **General** tab. What is the current dpi setting? What effect does changing the dpi setting to large size have?

_____

_____

■ Part D: Troubleshoot display settings

1. Open the **Display Properties** dialog box to the **Settings** tab.
2. Click the Troubleshoot button. The **Video Display Troubleshooter** page in the **Window XP Help and Support Center** opens (Figure 9-8).

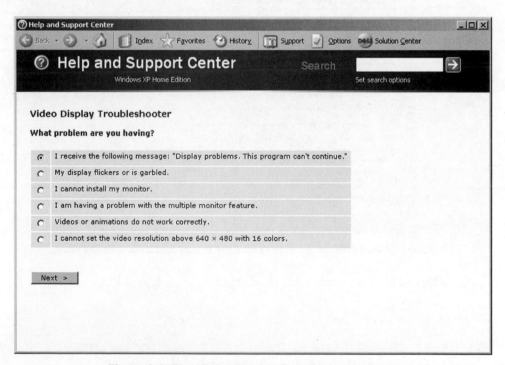

Figure 9-8: The Video Display Troubleshooter page

3. Choose a problem and review the support materials that Microsoft makes available to help troubleshoot that problem. Record the problem you chose and the information about solving the problem that you discovered below.

_____

_____

_____

Project 9.4	Selecting and Installing a Video Card
Overview	Video cards handle commands from the CPU and pass them to the monitor. The better the video card, the more smoothly your monitor will display video. Video cards are one of the most commonly upgraded components of a computer. In this project, you will use the web to research different types of video cards and gather information about them, and also practice installing a video card.
Outcomes	After completing this project, you will know how to: ▲ research and gather information about video cards ▲ install a video card
What you'll need	To complete this project, you will need: ▲ a Windows computer ▲ a video card ▲ access to the Internet
Completion time	60 minutes
Precautions	Be sure to have ESD materials available. If your PC has integrated video (in which case a monitor plugs into the motherboard, as opposed to a port on an expansion card) you will need to disable the onboard video. You can usually disable onboard video through the BIOS settings, or, on an older computer, by jumpers on the motherboard.

■ Part A: Select a video card

1. Open up a web browser and go to an online PC components retailer, such as Tiger Direct, Newegg.com or PC Connection. A web search for 'video cards' will also yield additional choices.

2. Choose three video cards from the website ranging in price from inexpensive to expensive and answer the following questions:

Video Card #1

Price:_____

Interface type (PCI, AGP):_____

3D APIs supported: _____

Memory type, size and interface:_____

Manufacturer: _____

Video Card #2

Price:_____

Interface type (PCI, AGP):_____

3D APIs supported: _____

Memory type, size and interface:_____

Manufacturer: _____

Video Card #3

Price:_____

Interface type (PCI, AGP):_____

3D APIs supported: _____

Memory type, size and interface:_____

Manufacturer: _____

3. Which video card do you think is the best general purpose card? Why?

    _____

    _____

    _____

4. Which video card do you think would be the best choice for business-computing needs? Why?

    _____

    _____

    _____

5. Which video card do you think would be the best choice for gaming? Why?

    _____

    _____

    _____

■ Part B: Install a video card

1. Shut down and the computer and unplug its power cable.
2. Remove the computer case cover. Be sure to use an antistatic wrist strap once the cover is off.
3. Locate an appropriate expansion slot for the video card.
4. Install the video card into the expansion slot and screw the card to the case (Figure 9-9). Make sure that the card is properly seated. An improperly seated card is a common cause of video problems.

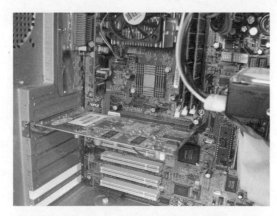

Figure 9-9: A properly installed video card

5. Connect the monitor card to the appropriate port on the video card.

6. Replace the PC's cover and plug the computer back in.

7. Power on the monitor and then power on the computer.

8. Windows should detect the new video card and install the appropriate drivers. If Windows does not automatically find the drivers, you will need to install them manually, through the **Add New Hardware Wizard** that opens, or by installing the manufacturer software that came with the video card.

Project 9.5	Installing and Configuring Dual Monitors
Overview	Installing dual monitors is a complicated but often extremely useful procedure. The added space provided by a second monitor enables you to accomplish more difficult tasks at your workstation. In this project, you will learn to install a dual monitor and configure your computer to handle a dual monitor setup.
Outcomes	After completing this project, you will know how to: ▲ install and configure a second monitor to your computer system
What you'll need	To complete this project, you will need: ▲ a Windows XP computer with an existing monitor, and available PCI and/or AGP slot ▲ a second monitor ▲ a PCI and/or AGP video adapter for the second monitor, or a multiple-display compatible video adapter ▲ a technician's toolkit with anti-static wrist strap
Completion time	60 minutes
Precautions	As always, take the necessary precautions to guard against ESD when opening up the computer.

■ Part A: Install dual monitors

1. Power on the PC.

2. After completing the startup and logon, verify that the current video system is working correctly. After the installation is complete, this will be the primary monitor.

3. Shut down the PC.

4. Disconnect the PC from external power sources.

5. Open the computer case.

6. Attach the antistatic wrist strap to a metal portion of the computer case.

7. Locate an available PCI or AGP slot.

8. Remove the slot cover from the back of the case. Keep the screw for securing the additional video card into the computer.

9. Insert the PCI or AGP video adapter into the slot and secure it into place using the screw from the slot cover.

10. Attach a monitor to the second video adapter.

11. Disconnect the antistatic wrist strap from the computer case. Do not replace the computer case cover at this time.

12. Attach external power to the computer system and, if necessary, both monitors.

13. Verify the driver installation instructions from the hardware manufacturer before continuing. Some vendors recommend that you cancel the **Add New Hardware Wizard** process and run a setup utility instead. In this case, you will cancel the **Add New Hardware Wizard** in Step 15.

14. Power on the computer system and both monitors.

15. During the boot process, the system should display on the primary (old) monitor. While booting, the system should detect the additional video adapter and access the **Add New Hardware Wizard**. If the manufacturer recommends canceling the **Add New Hardware Wizard** and running a setup utility instead, cancel the wizard at this step and skip to Step 17.

16. When the **Add New Hardware Wizard** prompts for the drivers disk which accompanies new monitors, insert the drivers disk into the drive and click Next. Follow the instructions to complete the driver installation.

17. After the video driver installation has completed, you might need to restart the system to activate both sets of video drivers.

18. After you have installed the second video adapter and monitor, your video system setup screen will have a new appearance. When a system has a single monitor, the **Settings** tab of the **Display Properties** dialog box appears with only one monitor in the window. When a system has more than one monitor, the **Settings** tab of the **Display Properties** dialog box tab appears with multiple monitors in the windows. If your system is showing both monitors, and an image is appearing on both monitors, then you have successfully installed a dual monitor system.

19. Open the **Control Panel**, and double-click the **Display** icon to open the **Display Properties** dialog box. Click the **Settings** tab. If the secondary monitor is not available on the **Settings** tab of the **Display Properties** dialog box, use the **Device Manager** to verify that Windows has detected the second monitor.

20. If Windows has not detected the additional video adapter, then verify that all adapters have support for multiple displays, especially if one of the adapters is integrated into the system board.

21. If the secondary adapter has been detected, but the monitor does not display, then perform the following troubleshooting steps:

    a. Verify that all adapters have support for multiple displays (especially if one of the adapters is integrated into the system board).

    b. Try changing the position of the adapters in the system board slots (this is only possible when using more than one like interface such as multiple PCI adapters).

c. Verify that the correct video driver has been installed. Select the monitor on the non-operating adapter by clicking on its image on the **Settings** tab in the **Display Properties** dialog box and then clicking on the check box for **Use this device as the primary monitor**. Click Apply to put this change into effect.

■ Part B: Configure the monitors to display the same desktop

1. From the **Settings** tab of the **Display Properties** dialog box, select the **secondary monitor**. To verify which monitor is the secondary monitor, right-click **Monitor 1** and select **Identify**. A **1** will appear on the screen of the primary monitor.

2. Place a checkmark next to **Extend My Windows Desktop onto This Monitor** (Figure 9-10. Click Apply. Making this selection allows you to view the same desktop across the monitors. Doing this, you can drag items from one monitor to the other or stretch windows to span monitors.

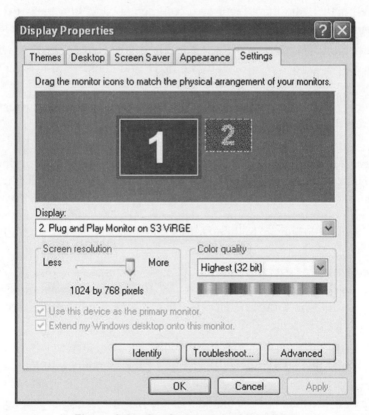

Figure 9-10: Configuring dual monitors

3. The display properties can be adjusted individually. When doing this, understand that the results of using different screen resolutions might be less than satisfactory. To adjust the settings for an individual monitor, click on the numbered monitor in the **Settings** tab and then adjust the **Colors** and **Screen Area** as you would for an individual monitor system.

4. After you are satisfied with the installation of the multiple monitor system, power down the PC, replace and secure the system cover, position the monitors as desired, and then restart the PC and test the monitors to verify that they are working correctly.

Project 9.6	Selecting and Installing a Sound Card
Overview	Installing a sound card in an expansion slot on the motherboard allows your computer to produce sound. Many situations can arise in which knowing how to install a sound card could be useful. For example, an older or malfunctioning sound card might need replacing, or perhaps a newer model might be more desirable for a cutting-edge computer user. In this project, you will use the web to research different types of sound cards and gather information about them and also practice installing a sound card.
Outcomes	After completing this project, you will know how to: ▲ research and gather information about sound cards ▲ install a sound card
What you'll need	To complete this project, you will need: ▲ a a sound card and associated Setup software ▲ a Windows XP computer ▲ for Part B, a Windows XP computer with two sound cards installed ▲ a technician's toolkit with antistatic wrist strap
Completion time	60 minutes
Precautions	As always, take the necessary precautions to guard against ESD when opening up the computer. Before installing the sound card, be sure to read the manufacturer's manual for any special configuration requirements.

■ Part A: Select a sound card

1. Open up a web browser and go to an online PC components retailer, such as Tiger Direct, Newegg.com, or PC Connection. A web search for 'sound cards' will also yield additional choices.

2. Choose three sounds cards from the website ranging in price from inexpensive to expensive and answer the following questions:

Sound Card #1

Price:_____

Number of bits:_____

Maximum sampling rate: _____

Harmonic distortion (THD +N):_____

Signal-to-noise ratio (SNR):_____

Manufacturer: _____

Sound Card #2

Price:_____

Number of bits:_____

Maximum sampling rate: _____

Harmonic distortion (THD +N):_____

Signal-to-noise ratio (SNR):_____

Manufacturer: _____

Sound Card #3

Price:_____

Number of bits:_____

Maximum sampling rate: _____

Harmonic distortion (THD +N):_____

Signal-to-noise ratio (SNR):_____

Manufacturer: _____

3. Which sound card do you think is the best general purpose card? Why?

_____

_____

_____

4. Which sound card do you think would be the best choice for entertainment? Why?

_____

_____

_____

■ Part B: Install a sound card

1. Turn off and unplug the computer.
2. Remove the computer's case cover and locate an empty expansion slot that is compatible with the card, preferably near the CD-ROM drive. Be sure to protect against ESD by using an antistatic wrist strap.
3. Remove the cover from the expansion slot opening in the back of the PC's case.
4. Install the sound card into the expansion slot and screw the card to the case.
5. Connect the sound card to the CD-ROM drive by using an audio cable.
6. Replace the computer's case cover and plug the computer back in.
7. Connect any external speakers and microphone to the appropriate ports.
8. Restart the computer. Windows will automatically detect the card and attempt to install appropriate drivers. However, for full functionality of your sound card, you will need to install any software that came with the sound card. To do this, you can cancel out of the **Add New Hardware Wizard** and run the manufacturer's setup software.

■ Part C: Select among multiple sound devices

Note: This part of the project assumes that two sound cards have been installed.

1. Open the **Control Panel** and double-click the **Sounds and Audio Devices** icon.

2. The **Sounds and Audio Devices Properties** dialog box will appear (Figure 9-11).

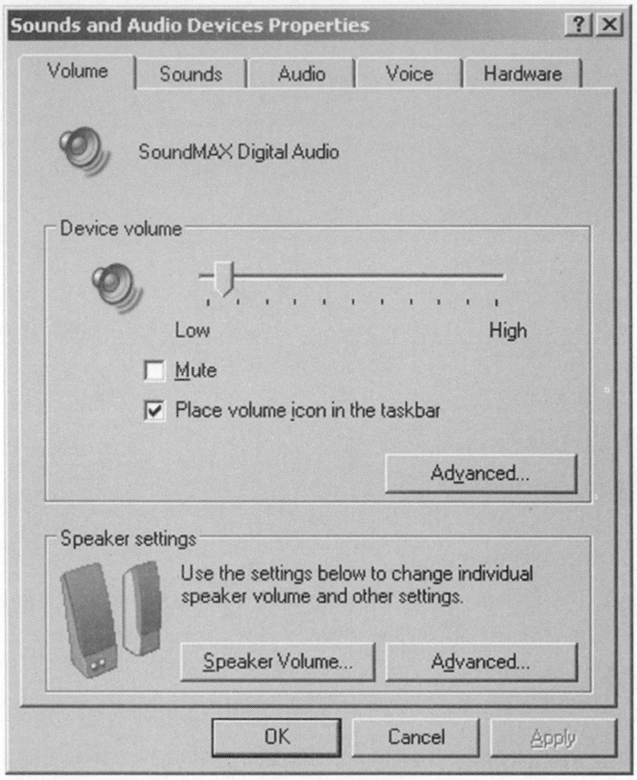

Figure 9-11: The Sounds and Audio Devices Properties dialog box

3. Select the Audio tab and open the drop-down lists in the **Sound playback**, **Sound recording**, and **MIDI music playback** sections. What devices are listed for each section?

_____

_____

_____

4. Select the preferred device for each section and click the OK button.

5. Select the **Voice** tab and open the drop-down lists in the **Voice playback** and **Voice recording** sections. What devices are listed for each section?

_____

_____

6. Select the preferred device for each section and click the OK button.

Project 9.7	Working with Other I/O Devices
Overview	There are a wide variety of other I/O devices that you will need to learn to work with. Two examples of these devices are digital scanners and digital cameras. In this project, you will learn how to connect these devices to your computer.
Outcomes	After completing this project, you will know how to: ▲ install other I/O devices
What you'll need	To complete this project, you will need: ▲ a flatbed scanner (Figure 9-12) ▲ a digital camera with a flash memory card containing pictures, and USB or FireWire cable ▲ a Windows computer
Completion time	30 minutes
Precautions	None

Figure 9-12: Flatbed scanner

■ Part A: Install a flatbed scanner

1. Check the scanner for a switch or pin that serves as a locking mechanism. Most scanners lock down the CCD for transport to prevent damage. If the unit has a lock, unlock it.

2. What type of port are you going to attach the scanner to?

   _____

3. If you're installing via a parallel or SCSI port, turn off your computer. If you're installing via a USB port, you can leave your computer on.

4. If connecting a SCSI scanner, make sure an appropriate SCSI adapter is installed in the PC. Install one if not.

5. Connect the scanner to the PC using the appropriate port.

6. Plug the scanner into an AC power outlet.

7. Turn your computer on, and then turn on the scanner.

8. Windows should recognize the new scanner and install the appropriate drivers. If prompted, insert the scanner's installation disk or CD at this step and follow the on-screen prompts.

9. If the scanner came with its own software, install that software.

■ Part B: Connect a digital camera

1. Connect the cable to the camera. Refer to the camera's manual if needed.

2. Turn on the camera.

3. If needed, flip any switches or press any buttons on the camera that put it into a PC interface mode. Refer to the camera's manual if needed.

4. Connect the cable to the PC, either to the USB or the FireWire port as appropriate.

5. Windows should recognize the camera's flash RAM card as a new drive and assign it a drive letter. Double-click that drive letter in **My Computer** to browse the pictures.

6. Use **My Computer** to transfer the pictures to your hard disk or other disk on your system.

7. Optionally, delete the pictures from the camera.

8. Disconnect the camera from the PC. Press any buttons or flip any switches on the camera needed to put it back into normal camera mode. Then turn it off.

10
PRINTERS

PROJECTS

Project 10.1	Printer and Printer Interfaces
Overview	The printer interface consists of the hardware interface and software (drivers) that support the printer. Popular hardware interfaces for printers include parallel, USB, and network interfaces. Printer drivers must be selected for the type, brand, and model of printer in use; the operating system installed; and the computer port to which the printer is attached. The printer driver controls the print process.
	In this project, you will gather information about your printer's interface in order to learn more about how your printer works.
Outcomes	After completing this project, you will know how to:
	▲ acquire information about a printer's interface
What you'll need	To complete this project, you will need:
	▲ a Windows XP computer with a printer installed
Completion time	30 minutes
Precautions	None

1. Boot to the CMOS and locate the settings for the serial (COM) and parallel ports. Do not make any changes to CMOS settings.

2. Record the settings for COM 1 and COM 2, if available, and the parallel port:

   Serial port address and IRQ settings: _____

   Parallel port address and IRQ settings: _____

   Parallel port mode: _____

3. Exist CMOS and log on to the Windows operating system.

4. Open the **Control Panel**, select **Administrative Tools**, then select **Computer Management**, and finally **Device Manager**.

5. In **Device Manager**, click the plus sign next to **Ports** (Figure 10-1).

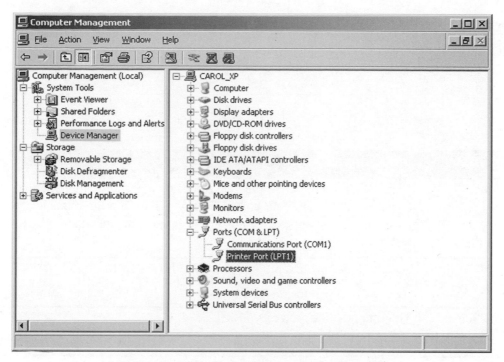

Figure 10-1: The Ports node in Device Manager

5. Right-click the **LPT** port and then click **Properties**. The **Printer Port (LPT1) Properties** dialog box opens (Figure 10-2).

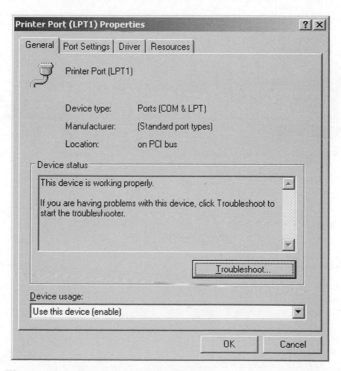

Figure 10-2: The Printer Port (LPT1) Properties dialog box

6. Select the **Resources** tab. Record the **IRQ** and **I/O address** for this port.

IRQ: _____

I/O Address: _____

Project 10.2	Installing a Printer
Overview	In this exercise, you will practice installing a printer without actually having a printer attached to your computer. If you have a printer attached, the procedure is the same, except that you can test the installation by printing a test page.
Outcomes	After completing this project, you will know how to: ▲ install a printer on a computer
What you'll need	To complete this project, you will need: ▲ a Windows XP computer
Completion time	30 minutes
Precautions	As with any project requiring you to open a computer, make sure to take the necessary precautions to guard against ESD. Also, back up your important data on your hard disk before you do any work on your computer.

1. Open the **Control Panel**, and select **Printers and Faxes** (Figure 10-3).

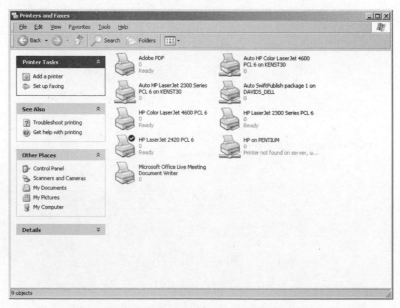

Figure 10-3: The Printer and Faxes window

2. Record any printers that appear in the **Printers and Faxes** window.

    _____

    _____

    _____

    _____

3. In the **Printers and Faxes** window, select **Add a Printer** to begin the installation.

4. The **Add Printer Wizard Welcome** page appears (Figure 10-4). Click Next.

Figure 10-4: The Add Printer Wizard Welcome page

5. The **Local or Network Printer** page appears (Figure 10-5). Select the **Local Printer Attached to This Computer** option. Clear the **Automatically detect** check box. Then click Next.

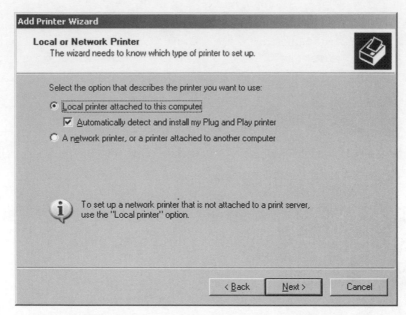

Figure 10-5: The Local or Network Printer page

6. The **Select a Printer Port** page appears (Figure 10-6). Select the **Use the Following Port— (LPT1)** option and click Next.

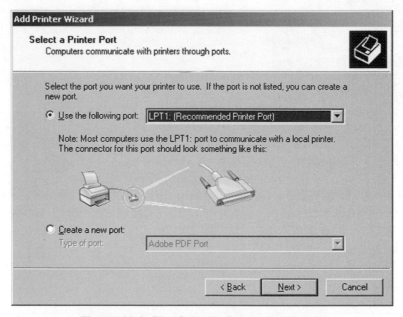

Figure 10-6: The Select a Printer Port page

7. The **Install Printer Software** page appears (Figure 10-7). Select a manufacturer and printer. In this instance, the choices do not matter, because you are not actually installing a real printer. If you were, you would select either the **Have Disk** button if you have a manufacturer-provided driver, or select the appropriate manufacturer and printer and allow Windows to provide you with access to the driver. Having the correct drivers for the printer involved is necessary in order to successfully install the printer. Click Next.

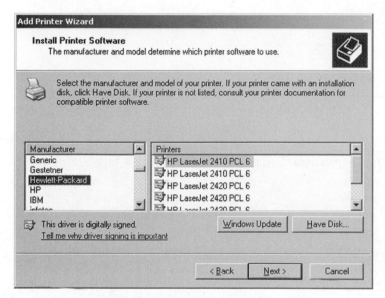

Figure 10-7: Install Printer Software page

8. The **Name Your Printer** page appears (Figure 10-8). Enter a name for the printer. Do not make the printer the default printer. Click Next.

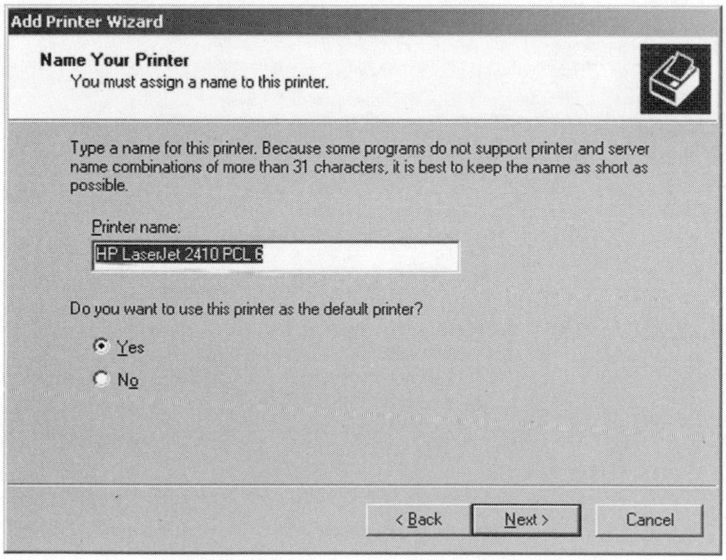

Figure 10-8: Name Your Printer page

9. The **Printer Sharing** page appears. Do not share the printer. Click Next.

10. The **Print Test Page** appears. Do not print a test page. Click Next.

11. Record the printer settings displayed in the **Completing the Add Printer Wizard** page below.

_____

_____

_____

_____

_____

12. Click Finish.

13. In the **Printer and Faxes** window, right-click the printer icon and select **Properties**.

14. In the **Printer Properties** dialog box, select the **Ports** tab (Figure 10-9). Is the printer you installed listed?

_____

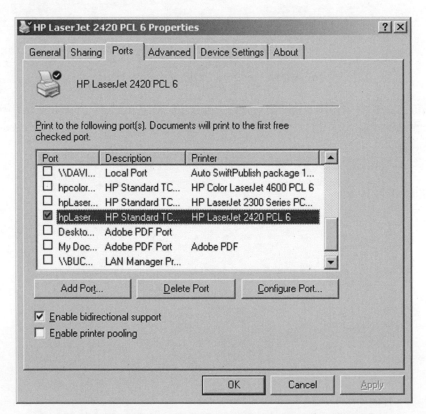

Figure 10-9: The Ports tab in the Printer Properties dialog box

Project 10.3	Connecting and Testing a Printer
Overview	In this project, you will perform the basic steps required to physically connect and test a printer. There are several ways in which a printer can connect to a computer, but most of these ways share the same steps.
Outcomes	After completing this project, you will know how to: ▲ connect and test a printer
What you'll need	To complete this project, you will need: ▲ a Windows XP or 2000 computer ▲ a printer
Completion time	30 minutes
Precautions	Once again, make sure to back up your hard drive before proceeding with this project, and take the necessary precautions to guard against ESD.

1. Review the manufacturer's installation instructions that came with your printer. Some printers (both parallel and USB) require that the drivers be installed prior to connecting the printer to the computer.

2. Unpack the printer and ready the printer for installation. You may need to remove packing tape, Styrofoam protectors, and attach components such as feed trays or ink or toner cartridges.

3. If any software setup programs must be run first before connecting the printer, do so now.

4. Check the printer manual to see if the printer has a separate self test that can be run before connecting the computer to the printer. A self-test checks that the printer is working correctly. If so, turn the printer on and follow the manufacturer's instructions for performing the self-test (Figure 10-10). Record the result.

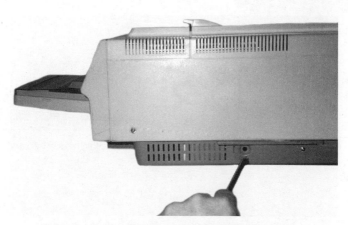

Figure 10-10: A laser printer's self-test button

5. If the printer connects with a parallel interface, turn the printer off.

6. Connect the necessary cables to connect the printer to the USB or parallel port.

7. Power on the printer, if it is off, and start up the computer. If you have already run a manufacturer's printer setup program, the printer driver is detected by Windows, installed, and configured automatically. Also, if your printer is Plug and Play compliant, Windows XP should install and configure the printer driver automatically. Otherwise, the **Found New Hardware Wizard** will open, giving the options of installing the printer software automatically or searching for printer drivers in a specific location. Follow the prompts of the **Found New Hardware Wizard** to install the printer software. Generally, it is better to have the driver installed automatically. If the Windows is unable to find a suitable driver, you may need to download a driver from the manufacturer's website, or run the manufacturer's Setup program to install the driver. Note that the screens and options differ slightly if the computer is running Windows 2000.

8. When the driver is successfully installed, you are prompted to print a test page. After a short period of time, another dialog box pops up, asking whether the print test was successful. If no print output appears, click to launch the Windows printer troubleshooter, which asks you a series of questions to help you diagnose the problem. If you are installing an inkjet printer, the wizard may prompt you to run a series of printer diagnostics to align the print heads and/or optimize color output with your display monitor.

9. The final screen of the **Found New Hardware Wizard** reports the status of the installation (Figure 10-11). Click Finish to complete the installation.

Figure 10-11: Completing the Found New Hardware Wizard

Project 10.4	Sharing a Printer
Overview	Often, it will be far more convenient to simply share a printer with a computer on a network than it would be to install that printer on each system. In this project, you will practice sharing a printer to another computer on a network.
Outcomes	After completing this project, you will know how to: ▲ share a printer
What you'll need	To complete this project, you will need: ▲ a computer with Windows XP installed ▲ a printer ▲ Windows XP installation CD ROM (for optional Steps 5–7)
Completion time	30 minutes
Precautions	None

1. Open the **Control Panel** and select **Printers and Faxes**.
2. Right-click on the icon of the printer you want to share and click **Sharing** on the shortcut menu to open the printer's **Properties** dialog box. Select the **Sharing** tab (Figure 10-12).

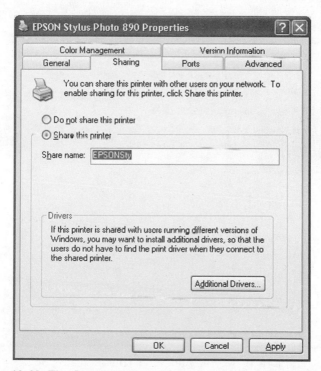

Figure 10-12: The Sharing tab in the Printer's Properties dialog box

4. Select the **Share this printer** option button. After doing this, the dialog box for entering the printer share name will become available. Windows will enter a variation of the printer's local name as the default share name. You may change the share name as desired.

Record the share name selected: _____

5. If you want add additional drivers that automatically download when users who are running different Windows operating systems first connect to the shared printer, click the Additional Drivers button (**Note:** Steps 5–7 cannot be completed without the Windows XP installation CD. If the CD is not available, skip to Step 8). This option allows you to force client computers to utilize drivers that are correct for your printer. This helps reduce the chance of a print job being sent to your printer that contains bad data or code and, as a result, locks the print queue.

6. An **Additional Drivers** dialog box opens (Figure 10-13). Note that the drivers for the operating system installed on the local computer already are selected. To add drivers for other operating systems, place a check mark for each operating system. If the only computers that will attach and use this shared printer run Windows XP and Windows 2000, then select only those drivers. If you select a driver that will never be used, then the disk space used for the driver will be wasted. If you leave off any driver for an operating system that will be used, then there is a chance a PC may use the wrong drivers.

Figure 10-13: The Additional Drivers dialog box

7. An **Insert Disk** dialog box will prompt you to download and save the drivers.

8. When you are returned to the **Sharing** tab in the **Printer Properties** dialog box, click Apply and then click OK.

9. The printer is now shared on the network. Any computer and user with access to your workgroup, and with rights on your computer, can now print to this printer across the network.

Project 10.5	Configuring and Managing Printers
Overview	There are a variety of tasks involved in configuring and managing a printer. You should know how to perform a variety of printing tasks such as pausing, resuming, and canceling printing, how to send documents to a different printer, how to specify the paper sizes for multiple paper trays, and how to set a separator page. In this project, you will practice performing these tasks.
Outcomes	After completing this project, you will know how to: ▲ pause, resume, and cancel printing ▲ send documents to a different printer ▲ specify the paper sizes for multiple paper trays ▲ set a separator page (a file that identifies a printed document, usually with the name of the user who requested it, and the date and time, that is printed between documents so that it is easy to identify the beginning and end of print jobs)
What you'll need	To complete this project, you will need: ▲ a Windows XP computer with a printer installed
Completion time	60 minutes
Precautions	Be sure to guard against ESD

■ Part A: Pause, resume, and cancel printing

1. Open the **Control Panel**, and select **Printer and Faxes**.
2. In the **Printer and Faxes** window, right-click the printer icon.

3. To pause printing, select the **Pause Printing** command. Notice that the word **Ready** under the **Printer** icon changes to **Paused** (Figure 10-14).

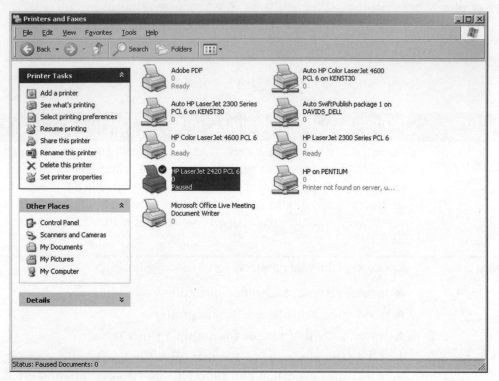

Figure 10-14: Pausing printing

4. To resume printing, right-click the printer icon again and select the **Resume Printing** command. The word **Ready** reappears under the printer icon.

5. To cancel all printing, right-click the printer icon, and select the **Cancel All Documents** command (Figure 10-15). (**Note:** This step assumes that you have sent a document to the printer; otherwise the **Cancel All Documents** command will not appear in the short-cut menu.) You can also access this command by double-clicking the printer icon and opening the **Printer** menu.

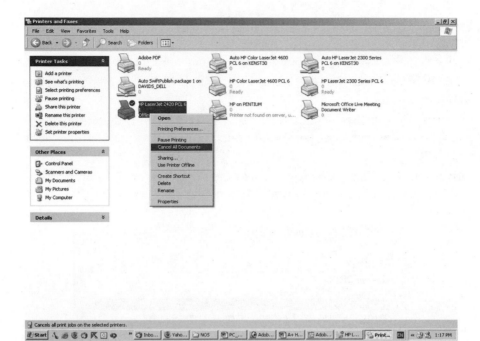

Figure 10-15: Canceling printing

6. To pause, resume, or cancel the printing of a specfic document, right-click the document in this window and select the appropriate command (Figure 10-16).

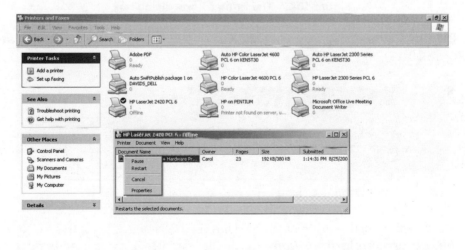

Figure 10-16: Pausing, restarting, or canceling the printing of a specific document

■ Part B: Send documents to a different printer

If a print device is malfunctioning, you might want to redirect print jobs to a different printer.

1. Open the **Printer and Faxes** window. Right-click the printer icon, and select the **Properties** command.

2. In the **Printer Properties** dialog box, select the **Ports** tab. If there is a working printer of the same type on another local port on the same printer server, select the check box for the port, and click OK.

3. Alternatively, if there is a working printer of the same type on a different print server, click the Add Port button to open the **Printer Ports** dialog box (Figure 10-17).

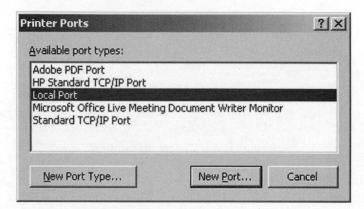

Figure 10-17: The Printer Ports dialog box

4. In the **Printer Ports** dialog box, click the New Port button to open the **Port Name** dialog box (Figure 10-18).

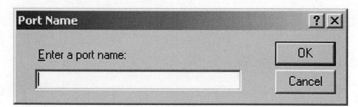

Figure 10-18: The Port Name dialog box

5. In the **Port Name** dialog box, enter the Universal Naming Convention (UNC) pathname (***printerservername**printername***) to the new printer in the **Enter a port name** text box.

■ Part C: Specify paper sizes for paper trays

1. Open the **Printer and Faxes** window. Right-click the printer icon and select the **Properties** command.

2. In the **Printer Properties** dialog box, select the **Device Settings** tab. Here, you can specify the paper size for each tray (Figure 10-19). Then, when the user selects a paper size, the print job is automatically routed to the correct paper tray. Click OK to close the dialog box.

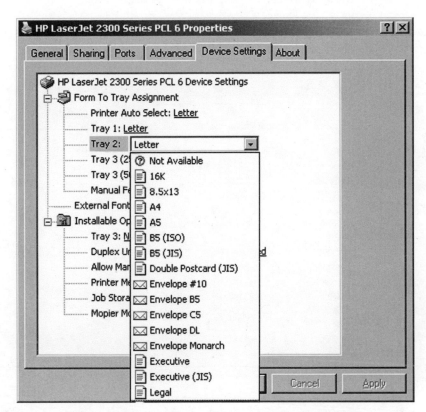

Figure 10-19: Specifying a paper size for a paper tray

■ Part D: Set a separator page

1. Open the **Properties** dialog box for the printer. Select the **Advanced** tab. Click the Separator Page button at the button of the dialog box.

2. The **Separator Page** dialog box opens (Figure 10-20).

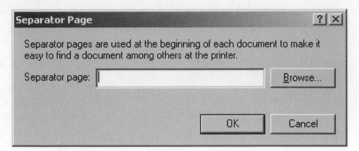

Figure 10-20: The Separator Page dialog box

3. Browse to locate the **SYSTEM32** folder where you will find four default separator pages from which to chose (Figure 10-21).

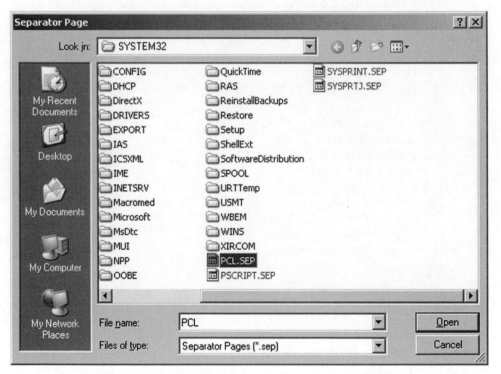

Figure 10-21: Locating the default separator page files

4. Select a file and click the Open button.
5. Click OK to close the **Separator Page** dialog box and **Properties** dialog box for the printer.

Project 10.6	Preventive Maintenance
Overview	Printers are notorious for being prone to malfunctioning and breaking. For this reason, it is extremely important that you understand how to perform maintenance on a printer to prevent any problems as best you can.
Outcomes	After completing this project, you will know how to: ▲ perform preventive maintenance on an inkjet printer ▲ set up a maintenance schedule for a laser printer
What you'll need	To complete this project, you will need: ▲ a Windows computer with an inkjet printer installed ▲ a Windows computer with a laser printer installed
Completion time	30 minutes
Precautions	None

■ Part A: Maintain an inkjet printer

1. Open the **Control Panel** and select **Printers and Faxes**. Right-click the icon of your inkjet printer and select click **Printing Preferences** from the shortcut menu.

2. Locate the maintenance functions for this printer (Figure 10-22). You will usually find these on a tab in the printer's **Properties** dialog box; although they may be installed as a separate utility function which you may find on the **Start** menu or as a shortcut on the desktop. Review the printer manual to see if any maintenance functions can be run by pressing buttons on the printer itself.

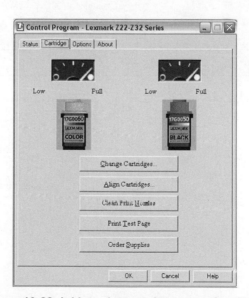

Figure 10-22: Inkjet printer maintenance functions

3. Run the maintenance programs.

4. Turn the printer's power off and then on again. Observe the printer to see if it performs any maintenance checks.

■ Part B: Maintain a laser printer

1. Use whatever resources are available to you to gather information about the maintenance schedule of your printer. Read the printer's documentation, or search online for your printer information. Answer the following questions:

   a. How can you tell the printer needs maintenance?

   _____

   b. Do you need any special cleaning tools? What are they, if so?

   _____

   c. Do you need to periodically remove sensitive parts for cleaning? Which ones, if so?

   _____

   d. Are there any other important suggestions for cleaning the printer?

   _____

2. Using the information you entered in Step 1, create a list of items you will need to clean your laser printer, and write down an appropriate schedule for when these items will be used.

   _____

   _____

   _____

   _____

   _____

Project 10.7	Comparing Printers
Overview	The vast variety of printers makes choosing an appropriate one for the home or the office a difficult task. In this project, you will use the Internet to research different printing options. Doing this should give you a better idea of which printer to recommend in a particular situation.
Outcomes	After completing this project, you will know how to: ▲ choose an appropriate printer
What you'll need	To complete this project, you will need: ▲ a computer with Internet access
Completion time	30 minutes
Precautions	None

1. Perform a web search for 'computer printers' and find an online retailer with a good selection of printers. If you can't find one with this method, try Tiger Direct, NewEgg.com, or CDW.

2. Pick three printers that use different print technologies (laser, inkjet, thermal, etc.) and record the following information about them:

Printer 1

Name: _____

Supports color printing: _____

Pages per minute: _____

Interface used: _____

Price: _____

Printer 2

Name: _____

Supports color printing: _____

Pages per minute: _____

Interface used: _____

Price: _____

Printer 3

Name: _____

Supports color printing: _____

Pages per minute: _____

Interface used: _____

Price: _____

3. Assume that you are the owner of a small business. You need a printer capable of printing non-color documents at high speeds. You don't want to pay extra for a printer that supports color printing if you can help it. Which of your three choices would be the best fit for you and why?

    _____

    _____

    _____

    _____

4. Assume that you want a printer for your home office. You want a printer capable of color printing, but you want to spend as little as possible on it. You plan to print about 100 color pictures each year. If possible, you would like a printer that uses the USB interface. Which of your three choices would be the best fit for you and why?

    _____

    _____

    _____

    _____

5. Assume that you are a division manager at a large publishing company. You need a workhorse printer capable of color printing at the highest speeds available. Price is not a concern. Which of your three choices would be the best fit for you and why?

    _____

    _____

    _____

    _____

11
PORTABLE SYSTEMS

PROJECTS

Project 11.1	Replacing a Laptop's Battery
Overview	All laptop batteries have a finite lifetime (typically about 2 years), and eventually must be replaced. It is a simple procedure of locating the battery's release mechanism and removing and replacing the existing battery. In this project, you will practice removing and replacing your laptop's batteries.
Outcomes	After completing this project, you will know how to: ▲ replace a laptop's battery
What you'll need	To complete this project, you will need: ▲ a laptop computer ▲ an appropriate laptop replacement battery ▲ the laptop's documentation
Completion time	60 minutes
Precautions	Be sure to guard against ESD. Also, some laptops may have a secondary battery pack used to extend battery life, which may be located in a modular drive bay. Consult your laptop manual to determine any specific mechanisms used for battery power.

1. First, make sure that the computer has been turned off, rather than being in hibernation mode.

2. Disconnect the AC power adapter from the laptop, and detach any external peripheral cables.

3. Locate the battery compartment. There are two common systems used for batteries. One system uses a hidden compartment where the battery is located behind a door on the laptop (Figure 11-1). On other systems, the battery may be a part of the bottom or side of the laptop but not located behind a cover. If necessary, consult the laptop documentation.

Figure 11-1: Battery compartment behind door

4. Where is the battery compartment on this laptop located?

    _____

5. Remove any panels needed to access the battery component.

6. Remove the battery. If the battery is located behind a compartment door, there will be a latch or screw securing the door. Remove the screw or push the latch to open the battery compartment. Generally, but not always, there will be some form of handle attached to the battery inside the compartment. Locate this handle, if any, and gently pull the battery out of the compartment. Batteries that form part of the side or bottom of the laptop are generally held in place with a latch. Usually this is a slide that releases the catch holding the battery in place. Locate this latch and press it in the direction indicated on the latch system. While holding the latch in the open position, locate the fingerhold on the battery. Gently pull up or push out on the fingerhold (depending on the location of the battery).

6. Insert the new battery and close the compartment door if necessary.

7. If you have inserted a new battery, connect the AC adapter to the laptop and leave the laptop turned off in order to fully charge the battery. Consult with the laptop's manual or battery's documentation to see how long the battery must be charged the first time.

8. When the new battery is finished charging, or if you are using a used battery, remove the AC adapter and turn the laptop on to confirm that the laptop is receiving power from the battery.

Project 11.2	Upgrading Laptop Memory
Overview	Upgrading memory is one of the more common procedures performed on laptops. It is also one of the simplest. In this project, you will practice upgrading a laptop's memory by removing the old memory and replacing it with a newer module.
Outcomes	After completing this project, you will know how to: ▲ upgrade a laptop's memory
What you'll need	To complete this project, you will need: ▲ a laptop computer ▲ an appropriate memory module (for the purposes of this project, you can also reinsert the old memory module instead) ▲ documentation for the laptop detailing how to remove and insert memory ▲ a technician's toolkit with a small Phillips head screwdriver for removing the cover over the memory panel on the laptop and an anti-static wrist strap
Completion time	30 minutes

Precautions	As with any project requiring you to open a computer, make sure to take the necessary precautions to guard against ESD. Also, back up your important data on your hard disk before you do any work on your computer.

■ Part A: Remove a memory module

1. Back up the data on the hard disk.

2. Turn off the computer (make sure that it is in fact turned off, rather than being in hibernation mode).

3. Disconnect the laptop from the AC power supply.

4. Place the laptop on a static free work surface. Use an antistatic wrist strap.

5. Remove the battery from the laptop (see Project 11.1).

6. Consult the laptop documentation to find out where the memory access panel is located is located (its location may differ depending the make and model of the laptop).

7. Remove the screw(s) that secure the memory access panel.

8. Look over the area under the memory access panel door. Locate the memory modules, memory slots and the catches that hold the memory modules into the slots.

9. Carefully press out away from the memory module on both catches at the same time until the module has been released. These slots are usually spring loaded. When the module has been released, it will pop up at an angle from the system board (Figure 11-2). Repeat this process for each installed memory module.

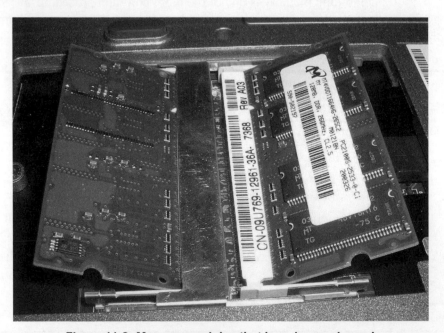

Figure 11-2: Memory modules that have been released

10. Carefully remove the memory module(s) out from the slots and place them on a clean, static-free surface. Do not stack a module on top of another.

11. The main types of laptop memory packages form factors are the 72-pin SoDIMM (Figure 11-3), the 144-pin SoDIMM, the 144-pin MicroDIMM (Figure 11-4), and the 160-pin RoDIMM.

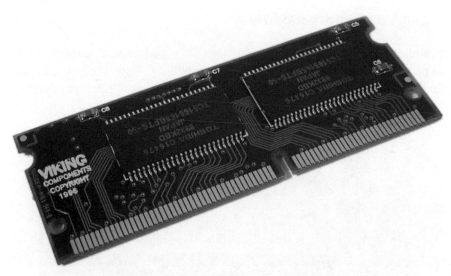

Figure 11-3: SoDIMM memory modules

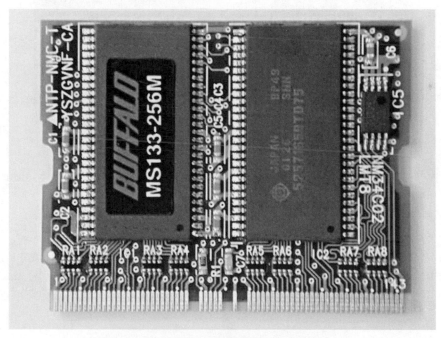

Figure 11-4: MicroDIMM memory module

12. What type of memory package does the laptop contain?

_____

■ Part B: Insert a memory module

1. Memory modules have a notch that should align with the key in a memory slot (Figure 11-5). This is to prevent the incorrect installation of the module. Align the notch in the module with the key in the slot and carefully press the module into the slot. Keep approximately the same angle as shown in Figure 11-2. Repeat this process for each additional memory module.

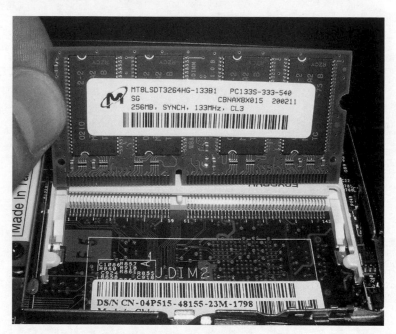

Figure 11-5: Memory module notches

2. Gently press down on the memory module until the catches hold the module down and in place. Repeat this process for each memory module.

3. Replace the memory access panel cover and secure it in place with screws.

4. Replace the battery and reattach the AC power supply to the system board.

5. Power on the laptop. If the amount of RAM has changed, the system should give a message during the boot process asking you to verify the change. You should only be alarmed by this message if the change was not expected or if the amount of memory reported is not what you expected. The laptop is now ready for use.

Project 11.3	Replacing a Hard Disk Drive in a Laptop
Overview	Another procedure commonly performed on laptops is upgrading the hard disk. There are many ways to improve your laptop's disk space, but in this project, you will learn how to remove your old hard disk and replace it with a different model.
Outcomes	After completing this project, you will know how to: ▲ install a hard disk drive in a laptop
What you'll need	To complete this project, you will need: ▲ a laptop computer ▲ an appropriate hard disk drive ▲ a bootable floppy disk to restart the PC after installing the new hard disk ▲ a technician's toolkit with a small Phillips-head screwdriver and flat-head screwdrivers to remove screws on access plates, if necessary and an anti-static wrist strap ▲ the laptop's documentation
Completion time	30 minutes
Precautions	Once again, make sure to back up your hard drive before proceeding with this project, and take the necessary precautions to guard against ESD. Also, make sure you refer to the laptop's documentation to determine how to access the hard disk drive.

1. Back up your important data on your hard disk and then turn off the laptop.
2. Disconnect the laptop from the AC power adapter, and place the laptop on a static free work surface. Use an antistatic wrist strap.
3. Remove the battery (see Project 11.1).
4. Locate the hard disk drive bay cover. If necessary, refer to the laptop's documentation to find out what you need to remove for access to the hard disk drive.
5. Remove the screw(s) that secure the cover.
6. Remove the existing hard drive. The exact method varies. Depending on the design of the particular system, you may need to complete Step a only, or you may need to complete both Steps a and b. You should be able to determine this as you proceed.
   a. Carefully remove the cover (Figure 11-6). The laptop user manual may say whether you need to lift and pull, just lift, or just pull. If this process also removes the hard disk drive from the bay, proceed to Step 7.

Figure 11-6: Hard Disk Drive Partially Removed

    b. If the cover is not attached to the hard disk drive, look for something that appears to be a handle (such as a piece of ribbon). Gently pull on this handle to remove the hard disk drive from the bay.

7. Observe how the various parts are attached to the hard disk drive. Carefully remove each of the items attached to the hard disk drive. Use care in removing any interface attachments so that the pins are not bent.

8. Carefully install each of the items removed in Step 6 onto the new hard disk drive.

9. Insert the drive back into the drive bay. It may require a small push to fully seat the drive in place.

10. If the cover is not attached to the hard disk drive, replace it and secure the cover the screw(s) you previously removed the bay cover.

11. Reinstall the laptop's battery (see Project 11.1 for additional details).

12. Attach the laptop to the AC power adapter.

13. At this point, the hardware is ready to be used. It should be noted, however, that under ordinary circumstances, it is necessary, at this point in the process, to partition the hard disk drive and install an operating system. To do so, boot the computer from your floppy startup disk, format the new drive, and install the operating system.

Project 11.4	Configuring Laptop Power Options
Overview	Windows XP supports two power management standards: Advanced Power Management (APM) and Advanced Configuration and Power Interface (ACPI). Most laptops today are configured with ACPI. APM is a legacy technology. In Windows XP and Windows 2000, you configure power management settings via the Power Options Properties dialog box, which you access from the Power Options icon in the Control Panel. You can configure when and whether the laptop can be put into standby or hibernate mode, and also configure settings for turning off power to the monitor or hard drives after defined times of inactivity. You can also configure the triggering of various alarms when battery power dips below a certain level.
Outcomes	After completing this project, you will know how to: ▲ configure power options on a laptop
What you'll need	To complete this project, you will need: ▲ a laptop computer with Windows XP installed
Completion time	30 minutes
Precautions	None

1. Open the **Control Panel** and double-click the **Power Options** icon to open the **Power Options Properties** dialog box.
2. On the **Power Schemes** tab, select **Portable/Laptop** in the **Power schemes** drop-down list (Figure 11-7)

Figure 11-7: Power Options Properties dialog box

3. In the **Settings for Portable/Laptop power scheme** section, open the drop down lists for **Turn off monitor**, **Turn off hard drive**, **System standby**, and **System hibernates** and select a time period for each. Record your selections below.

_____

_____

_____

_____

4. Click the Save As button. The **Save Scheme** dialog box opens. Choose and record a name for the power scheme in the **Save this power scheme as** text box.

_____

5. Click OK to close the **Save Scheme** dialog box, then click Apply in the **Power Options Properties** dialog box.

6. Reopen the drop-down list in the **Power schemes** section to make sure that the scheme you saved now appears on the list.

7. Select the **Alarms** tab. What is the **Low battery alarm** set at? What is the **Critical battery alarm** set at?

_____

_____

8. Set both at **25%** by moving the slider bar.

9. Click the Alarm Action button in the **Critical battery alarm** section to open the **Critical Battery Alarm Actions** dialog box (Figure 11-8).

Figure 11-8: The Critical Battery Alarm Actions dialog box

10. What notifications and actions are selected in this dialog box?

_____

_____

11. Select the **Power Meter** tab. Select the **Show details for each battery** check box, and then click the battery icon to open the **Detailed Information for Battery** dialog box.

12. Record the information you find in this dialog box below.

_____

_____

13. Close all open dialog boxes and windows.

Project 11.5	Installing and Removing PC Cards
Overview	Before installing a PC card, you must first consider the position of the card in the computer's PC card slots. Some laptops have only one PC card slot, but many have two, one immediately above the other. Additionally, there are several types of PC card slots. The primary slots are Type I, II, and III. The slots are generally backward compatible but not forward-compatible. For example, a type II slot may be able to service Type I PC cards, but a Type I slot is not able to service a Type II PC card.

There are also different ways used to connect external devices to the PC card. Figure 11-9 shows three cards. The card on the left uses a cord (dongle) to connect to external devices. The card in the middle connects using an X-jack. With this type of jack, a regular cord (usually LAN or phone line) connects into a small jack that pops out from the end of the PC card. The PC card on the right extends outside of the PC card slot to provide additional space for the connection. In the case of the card pictured, the additional length is largely for the purpose of providing space for an antenna—the card is a wireless LAN adapter.

Weighing the factors of position and type of slot, and connection type and PC card type of the card, you must decide the best position for installing the card. You also must remember that there may be future card installations (unknown cards) when making this decision. Only after considering these factors are you ready to install the PC card into the laptop. |
| Outcomes | After completing this project, you will know how to:

▲ install and remove PC cards in a laptop |

What you'll need	To complete this project, you will need:
	▲ a laptop computer with Windows XP installed
	▲ a PC card
	▲ a technician's tool kit and antistatic wrist strap
Completion time	30 minutes
Precautions	Be sure to guard against ESD.

Figure 11-9: PC Cards

■ Part A: Install a PC Card

1. Based on the connector type, card type, available slot types and other cards that may be installed in the PC card slots, select a location for the PC card.

2. Power on and logon to the laptop.

    Note: You can also install the PC card before turning the laptop on. A PC card is, however, hot-pluggable, and is designed to plug in while the laptop is powered on. Therefore, inserting a PC card while the system is running is a normal operation.

3. After the startup and logon procedures have all completed, carefully insert the PC card into the slot selected in Step 1.

4. After the card has been inserted, the **Found New Hardware Wizard** will open, which will load the necessary drivers for the device. If the drivers are not a part of the operating system, you will be prompted to provide a drivers disk during this operation.

5. Due to the nature of some cards (such a some modems and LAN adapters) it may be necessary to restart Windows for all settings to take effect. If you are prompted to restart the system, save all data, close all windows and restart the laptop before continuing.

6. After installing the PC card and restarting the system, you should test the device. To test the hardware, utilize its primary function. For example, it the PC card is a sound card, attach some speakers to the card and play a sound file. If the card successfully fulfills this function, it is working correctly.

■ Part B: Remove a PC Card

1. To unplug or eject hardware using the **Safely Remove Hardware** icon (the last icon on the right in Figure 11-10), double-click on the icon on the taskbar to open a dialog box listing the devices that may be removed from the system.

   Note: If you cannot find this icon on your taskbar, it may be hidden when inactive. To activate it, right-click within the taskbar's notification area, and then click Properties to open the **Taskbar and Start Menu Properties** dialog box. On the **Taskbar** tab, click Customize to open the **Customize Notifications** dialog box. Scroll down the list until you find **Safely Remove Hardware**, and in the **Behavior** column, open the drop-down list and change the behavior to **Always show**.

Figure 11-10: The Safely Remove Hardware icon

2. Select the device you wish to remove from the list presented to you in the dialog and, if necessary, click Next.

3. A confirmation dialog box appears. Verify that the device listed is correct and then click OK.

4. You will now see a prompt to remove the hardware from the system.

5. To remove a PC card from the laptop, press the eject button located next to the PC card slot. On many laptops, the computer will beep as the device is ejected.

Project 11.6	Comparing Laptops
Overview	Buying a laptop can be a difficult experience due to the vast variety of specifications and uses that laptops can have. Some laptops are designed for portability alone, some are designed for high performance, and some attempt to find a middle ground between the two extremes. In this project, you will compare laptops to help you make appropriate recommendations given particular situations.
Outcomes	After completing this project, you will know how to: ▲ select a laptop appropriately
What you'll need	To complete this project, you will need: ▲ a computer with Internet access
Completion time	60 minutes
Precautions	None

1. Perform a web search for 'laptops' or 'portable computers.' It should be fairly easy to find an online retailer of laptops. If you can't find a suitable one, try Tiger Direct, Dell, Hewlett Packard, or Amazon.

2. Pick three laptops and record the following specifications: name, processor information (brand and class), memory size, hard disk capacity, CD/DVD drive/burner, graphics card, monitor size, weight, and price:

Laptop 1

Name: _____

Processor: _____

Memory: _____

Hard disk: _____

CD/ DVD drive/burner: _____

Graphics card: _____

Monitor size: _____

Weight: _____

Price: _____

Laptop 2

Name: _____

Processor: _____

Memory: _____

Hard disk: _____

CD/ DVD drive/burner:_____

Graphics card: _____

Monitor size: _____

Weight: _____

Price: _____

Laptop 3

Name: _____

Processor: _____

Memory: _____

Hard disk: _____

CD/ DVD drive/burner:_____

Graphics card: _____

Monitor size: _____

Weight: _____

Price: _____

4. Assume that your work requires you to travel and that you need a new laptop to perform simple tasks like word processing and e-mail. Portability is most important to you, so a machine with a light weight and small monitor size would be ideal. If possible, you would like to minimize the price at the expense of your system's performance. Which of your three choices is best for you and why?

    _____

    _____

    _____

    _____

5. Assume that you are a gamer or computer enthusiast looking for a laptop that rivals the power of desktop PCs. You are willing to pay a high price for a laptop with a powerful processor and lots of memory and disk space. Which of your three choices is best for you and why?

    _____

    _____

    _____

    _____

6. Assume that you want a laptop to use for work at home. Portability is not as important to you as cost and performance. You would like a middle-of-the-road machine that is capable of smoothly performing common office tasks. Which of your three choices is best for you and why?

    _____

    _____

    _____

    _____

12

NETWORK FUNDAMENTALS

Project 12.1	Identifying Network Topologies
Overview	A *topology* describes the general layout of the network connections. LANs use several types of physical topologies (cable connection variations) and logical topologies (how the network messages travel). There are five primary topologies (some of which can be both logical and physical): bus, star, ring, mesh, and hybrid. A bus topology is the simplest physical topology. It consists of a single cable that runs to every workstation. Bus topology cabling systems (such as Ethernet) are the least expensive to install. However, if any one of the cables breaks, the entire network is disrupted. In a physical star topology, a cable is run from each workstation to a central device (a hub or switch), which is usually placed in a central location in the office (such as a utility closet). Star topologies are more expensive to install than bus networks, because several more cables need to be installed as well as the hubs. However, star networks are easy to configure and have a higher fault tolerance (one cable failing does not bring down the entire network). In a physical ring topology, stations are connected in a circle and use a unidirectional transmission path where messages move from workstation to workstation. Unlike a star topology network, the ring topology network will be disrupted if one entity is removed from the ring. Physical ring topology systems are not used commonly today because the hardware involved is fairly expensive and the fault tolerance is low. The mesh topology is the simplest logical topology in terms of data flow, but it is the most complex in terms of physical design. In this physical topology, each device is connected to every other device. This topology is rarely found in LANs, mainly because of the complexity of the cabling. Although a mesh topology has high fault tolerance, it is very expensive to install and maintain. In a logical mesh topology, there are multiple ways to get the data from source to destination. The data may not be able to take the direct route, but it can take an alternate, indirect route. The hybrid topology is simply a mix of the other topologies. Most networks today are both hybrid and also heterogeneous (they include a mix of components of different types and brands). The hybrid network may be more expensive than some types of network topologies, but it makes use of the best features of all the other topologies.
Outcomes	After completing this project, you will know how to: ▲ describe the advantages and disadvantages of various network topologies ▲ sketch examples of each topology

What you'll need	To complete this project, you will need:
	▲ the worksheet below
Completion time	30 minutes
Precautions	None

1. Describe the following topologies and list their advantages and disadvantages:

   a. Bus topology:

   _____

   _____

   _____

   _____

   b. Star topology:

   _____

   _____

   _____

   _____

   c. Ring topology:

   _____

   _____

   _____

   _____

   d. Mesh topology:

   _____

   _____

   _____

   _____

   e.   Hybrid topology:

_____

_____

_____

_____

2. Draw an example of a bus topology.

_____

3. Draw an example of a ring topology.

_____

4. Draw an example of a star topology.

Project 12.2	Identifying Installed Network Protocols
Overview	Identifying the network protocols installed on a computer is an important skill when troubleshooting network problems. In this project, you will learn where to find this information.
	There are four major network protocols are in use today: TCP/IP, IPX/SPX, NetBIOS, and AppleTalk.
	Transmission Control Protocol/Internet Protocol (TCP/IP) is the protocol suite used on the Internet. In order for any workstation or server to communicate with the Internet, it must have TCP/IP installed. Most networks today use TCP/IP as their networking protocol.
	The Internetwork Packet Exchange/Sequenced Packet Exchange (IPX/SPX) is the default communications protocol for versions of the Novell NetWare operating system before NetWare 5. It is often used with Windows networks as well, but in Windows networks, the implementation of the IPX/SPX protocol is known as NWLINK.

	NetBIOS (Network Basic Input Output System) is a session-layer network protocol that links a network operating system with specific network hardware. It is an application programming interface (API), not a full networking suite. It uses unique 15-character names that are periodically broadcast over the network so the names can be cataloged by the Network Neighborhood function. NetBIOS names are the names that show up in Windows Network Neighborhood. Many Windows computers use NetBIOS over TCP/IP. AppleTalk is both a protocol and a proprietary network architecture for Macintosh computers.
Outcomes	After completing this project, you will know how to: ▲ identify the network protocols installed on a computer
What you'll need	To complete this project, you will need: ▲ a Windows XP or Windows 2000 client computer
Completion time	30 minutes
Precautions	None

1. To examine the protocols installed on a Windows XP computer, open the **Control Panel** and select **Network Connections**.

2. In the **Network Connections** window, right-click **Local Area Connection**, choose **Properties**, and click the **General** tab (Figure 12-1).

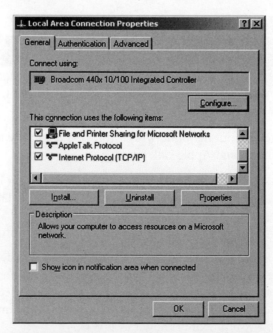

Figure 12-1: The General tab in the Local Area Connection Properties dialog box

3. Record the network card installed: _____

4. Record the information about the network protocols installed below (indicated by a check in the check box next to the name of the protocol).

_____

_____

_____

_____

5. Click each network protocol installed (such as **Internet Protocol (TCP/IP)**) and then click the Properties button to display the **Properties** dialog box for the protocol. Record the information you see there below for each protocol and then close the **Properties** dialog box for the protocol.

_____

_____

_____

_____

6. Now, click the Install button in **Local Area Connection Properties** dialog box to open the **Select Network Component Type** dialog box (Figure 12-2).

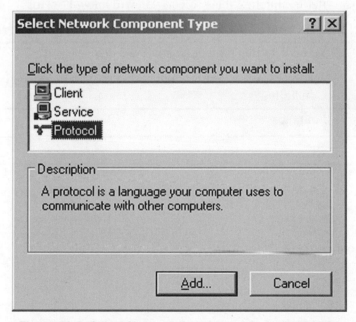

Figure 12-2: Select Network Component Type dialog box

7. Select **Protocol** and click the Add button to open the **Select Network Protocol** dialog box. Record the protocols you see listed there.

_____

_____

_____

Note: Any protocol that is already installed will not be listed here.

8. When you have finished, close the **Select Network Protocol** dialog box and any other open dialog boxes and windows and turn off the computer.

Project 12.3	Determining a MAC Address
Overview	Every NIC or network adapter is assigned a unique ID (called the MAC address) by its manufacturer when it is made. This address is burned into the NIC's firmware and cannot be changed. The MAC address is the basis for all network addressing, and all other address types are cross-referenced to it. A MAC address is a 48-bit address that is expressed as 12 hexadecimal digits (a hex digit is comprised of 4 bits), as in: *44-45-53-54-00-00*. In this project, you will learn how to determine the MAC address for a computer's NIC.
Outcomes	After completing this project, you will know how to: ▲ determine the MAC address for a network adapter
What you'll need	To complete this project, you will need: ▲ a Windows XP computer with a network interface card (NIC) installed
Completion time	10 minutes
Precautions	None

1. Turn on the computer, open the **Start** menu and then select **Run** to open the **Run** dialog box.
2. Type **cmd** in the **Open** field to open a **Command Prompt** window.
3. At the command prompt, type **ipconfig /all**.

4. You should see a heading titled **Ethernet adapter Local Area Connection**. The MAC address of your NIC is displayed in the **Physical Address** line (Figure 12-3).

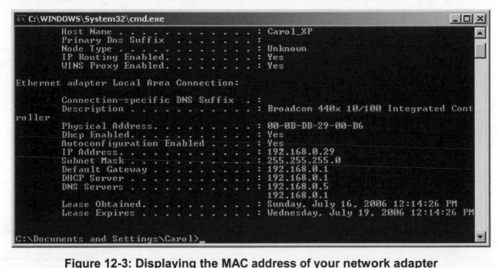

Figure 12-3: Displaying the MAC address of your network adapter

5. Record the MAC address: _____

6. The manufacturer of the NIC should be listed in the **Description** line.

_____

7. You can also use the command line utility **getmac** to return MAC address and to list network protocols associated with each address on the local computer or on other network computers. At the command prompt, type **getmac** (Figure 12-4). Figure 12-4 the shows the hexadecimal address. You can also use various parameters to obtain addresses of network computers.

Figure 12-4: Getmac

Project 12.4	Comparing Network Interface Cards (NICs)
Overview	A network interface card (NIC) is a card you install in your computer to connect, or interface, your computer to the network. This device provides the physical, electrical, and electronic connections to the network media. A NIC is either an expansion card or built in to the motherboard of the computer. Picking out an appropriate NIC can be a tricky process. In this project, you will familiarize yourself with the various specifications of NICs and learn to make appropriate recommendations given certain information.
Outcomes	After completing this project, you will know how to: ▲ select the most appropriate NIC for a given situation
What you'll need	To complete this project, you will need: ▲ a computer with Internet access
Completion time	60 minutes
Precautions	None

1. Do a web search for "network card" or "network adapter" or "NIC." When you have found a suitable online retailer, pick three network cards and record the following information about them:

   Card 1

   Name: _____

   Interface: _____

   Port type: _____

   Data transfer rate: _____

   Protocols supported: _____

   Price: _____

Card 2

Name: _____

Interface: _____

Port type: _____

Data transfer rate: _____

Protocols supported: _____

Price: _____

Card 3

Name: _____

Interface: _____

Port type: _____

Data transfer rate: _____

Protocols supported: _____

Price: _____

2. Assume that you require a NIC capable of transmitting data at very high speeds. Specifically, you need a NIC capable of transmitting speeds at a rate of 1000 Mbps. Which of your three choices would be best for you and why?

_____

_____

_____

_____

3. Assume that you need a NIC that is compatible with as many different protocols as possible. Which of your three choices would be best for you and why?

_____

_____

_____

_____

4. Assume that you are looking for a cost-effective NIC for your home network. You want to spend as little as possible and you're willing to sacrifice some speed to do so. Which of your three choices would be best for you and why?

_____

_____

_____

_____

Project 12.5	Installing a NIC
Overview	Installing a NIC is often necessary to connect a computer to a network. In this project, you will practice installing a NIC on a system.
Outcomes	After completing this project, you will know how to: ▲ install a NIC
What you'll need	To complete this project, you will need: ▲ a Windows XP computer with an available expansion slot ▲ a NIC ▲ a technician's tool kit and antistatic wrist strap
Completion time	60 minutes
Precautions	Be sure to guard against ESD

1. If necessary, shut down your computer system. Disconnect the power cord from the back of the computer system and carefully remove the case cover.
2. Attach the antistatic wrist strap to a metal portion of the computer case.
3. Locate an empty slot on the motherboard that fits your NIC. Most NICs fit into a PCI (Peripheral Component Interconnect) slot.
4. Remove the bracket from the computer case.
5. Carefully insert the NIC into the open slot.
6. Attach the NIC using a computer case screw.
7. Remove the antistatic wrist strap.
8. Replace the case cover and reattach the power cord to the computer system. Power on the computer.

9. The PnP features of Windows XP will detect new hardware at startup. In Windows XP, the startup process should detect the PCI network adapter (Figure 12-5) and launch the **Found New Hardware Wizard**.

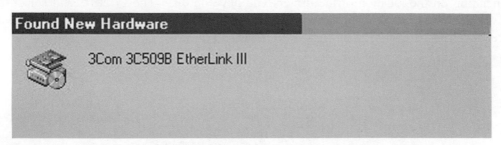

Found New Hardware

3Com 3C509B EtherLink III

Figure 12-5: New hardware found

10. The **Found New Hardware Wizard** should detect the device, install the drivers from the Windows drivers set, and complete default configuration settings automatically.

11. If the device driver is not part of the Windows drivers set, then the **Wizard** should still detect the device and list the device by type, name, and model. Click Next to continue.

12. The **Wizard** prompts you for the location of the device drivers. Choose to allow Windows to search for the best driver. If necessary, select the radio button for this option and click Next (Figure 12-6).

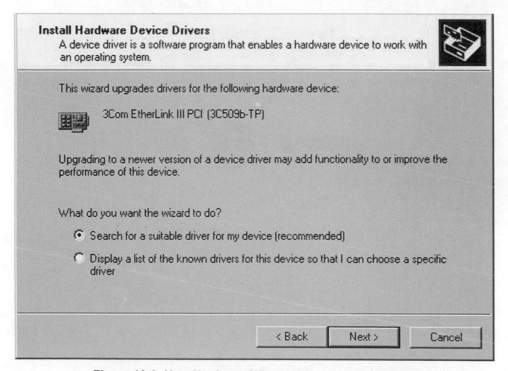

Install Hardware Device Drivers
A device driver is a software program that enables a hardware device to work with an operating system.

This wizard upgrades drivers for the following hardware device:

3Com EtherLink III PCI (3C509b-TP)

Upgrading to a newer version of a device driver may add functionality to or improve the performance of this device.

What do you want the wizard to do?

○ Search for a suitable driver for my device (recommended)

○ Display a list of the known drivers for this device so that I can choose a specific driver

< Back   Next >   Cancel

Figure 12-6: New Hardware Wizard driver search options

13. The **Wizard** now displays a list of locations that Windows will search for the proper device driver, including the operating system driver database. To narrow the search, select the floppy drive, CD-ROM drive, and/or Specify Location (browse to the location) radio buttons depending on the location of the drivers you have on disk. The **Wizard** will select the best driver either on the disk or from the operating system driver database. After making the selections for driver locations, click Next (Figure 12-7).

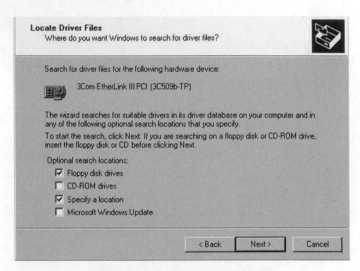

Figure 12-7: Search locations

14. The **Wizard** displays the driver selected. If you are not satisfied with the selection, use the back button to return to previous screens. If the driver selected is acceptable, click Next (Figure 12-8).

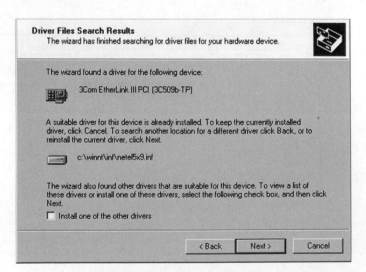

Figure 12-8: Search results

15. The completes the installation of the device drivers and displays a dialog box indicating that the device installation is complete. Click Finish .

Project 12.6	Installing a Wireless NIC
Overview	In a wireless network, computers and other devices communicate over radio frequencies instead of cables. Wireless transmission is broadcast essentially outward from the wireless device (instead of from point to point as in a cable), and wireless networks do not need to be connected in a certain topology. However, wireless devices in a network do communicate in one of two ways: In ad-hoc mode or infrastructure mode. In ad hoc mode, devices with wireless NICs communicate directly to each other. In infrastructure mode, each wireless device connects to a wireless access point. (WAP). WAPs allow wireless networks to be built as extensions of wired networks. In most respects, a wireless NIC (Figure 12-9) is the same as a traditional NIC, but instead of having a socket to plug a cable into, the wireless NIC has a radio antenna. On laptops with built-in wireless networking, this antenna may be internal. Wireless antennas act as both transmitters and receivers. The WAP is essentially a wireless bridge (or switch, as multiple end devices can connect simultaneously). It operates by connecting wireless clients together. In addition, it can connect those wireless clients to a wired network. As with a bridge or switch, the WAP indiscriminately propagates all broadcasts to all wireless and wired devices while allowing filtering based on MAC addresses. The WAP contains at least one radio antenna that it uses to communicate with its clients via radio frequency (RF) signals. The WAP can (depending on software settings) act as either an access point, which allows a wireless user transparent access to a wired network, or a wireless bridge, which will connect a wireless network to a wired network yet only pass traffic it knows belongs on the other side.
Outcomes	After completing this project, you will know how to: ▲ install a wireless NIC
What you'll need	To complete this project, you will need: ▲ Windows XP Professional computer with an available expansion slot ▲ a technician's tool kit and antistatic wrist strap ▲ PCI wireless LAN adapter ▲ an active wireless LAN access point ▲ Optionally, a laptop with a PC Card wireless LAN adapter may also be used for this project
Completion time	60 minutes
Precautions	Be sure to guard against ESD.

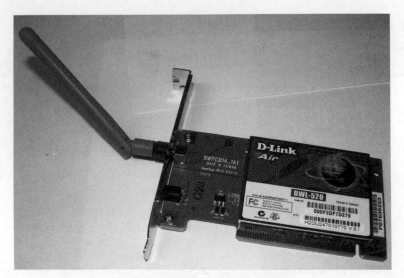

Figure 12-9: A wireless NIC

1. Remove the NIC from any packaging it may be in and unscrew the antenna from the card, if necessary.

2. Follow the steps in Project 12.5 to install the NIC. Note that once you have installed the NIC (and replaced and secured the PC cover), you must attach the screw-on antenna, if the NIC has one, from the outside at the back of the system. Make sure other items at the back of the computer to do not obstruct the antenna.

3. Once the NIC has been detected by Plug and Play and its drivers installed, you now configure the NIC to connect to the wireless access point.

4. Open the **Control Panel**. Select **Network and Internet Connections** to open the **Network and Internet Connections** window (Figure 12-10).

Figure 12-10: Windows XP Network and Internet Connections

5. In the **Network and Internet Connections** window, select **Network Connections** and then locate and right-click the icon for your wireless LAN connection.

6. Click **Properties** on the shortcut menu to open the adapter's **Properties** dialog box (Figure 12-11).

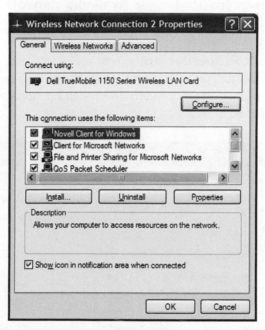

Figure 12-11: Windows XP Wireless Network Connection Properties dialog box

7. Select the **Wireless Networks** tab (Figure 12-12).

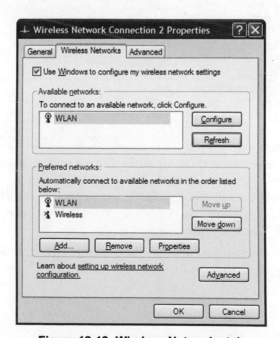

Figure 12-12: Wireless Networks tab

8. If the wireless network you will be using is listed in the **Preferred networks** list box, select it, click Properties and skip to Step 11.

9. If the wireless network you will be using is not in the **Preferred networks** list box, select the available wireless network listed in the **Available networks** list box. If there are no available networks listed, or if the network you are looking for is not listed, click the Refresh button. Click Configure.

10. The **Wireless Network Properties** dialog box will open. Enter the network name in the **Network Name (SSID)** text box (Figure 12-13). Select the data encryption type on the **Data encryption** drop-down menu (usually WEP), and if necessary, enter the network key in the **Network key** text box.

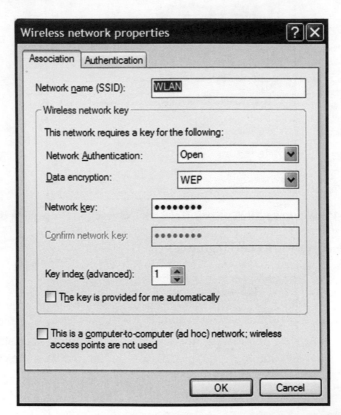

Figure 12-13: Windows XP authentication and network encryption key entry

10. Select the **Authentication** tab and configure any necessary **Authentication** settings. For example, the wireless LAN might use IEEE 802.1x for authentication. These settings are used with additional security devices, such as smart cards.

11. Close all open dialog boxes and windows. The wireless NIC is now configured. You should be able to begin using the network now.

Project 12.7	Planning a Network
Overview	The type of network you implement at home or at an organization will depend on the needs, requirements, budget, and capabilities at the organization. Several elements that you must determine in planning a network include: • The geographical extent of the network (WAN, LAN, PAN) and the number of computers and other devices that will be networked. • The resource access model (client/server or peer-to-peer) and the number of servers (if any) that will be needed. • The type of media that will be used (primarily Ethernet and/or wireless) In this exercise, you will review several different types of situations and determine the most appropriate type of network to implement.
Outcomes	After completing this project, you will know how to: ▲ plan a network
What you'll need	To complete this project, you will need: ▲ the worksheeet below
Completion time	30 minutes
Precautions	None

You are planning two networks:

A. A network for a family that has two desktop PCs and a laptop. The family also has two printers: a color laser printer and an inkjet.

B. A network for an new real estate agency that will employ six estate agents, and two clerical workers. Each employee uses a desktop PC and requires use of a printer.

For each of the networks, determine the type of network most suited to the situation, the hardware you anticipate being needed, and draw a sketch of how the computers will be connected together. Record your information below.

Network A:

Resource access model:

_____

Geographical extent:

_____

Transmission media:

_____

Topology:

_____

Hardware:

_____

_____

_____

_____

_____

_____

Network sketch:

_____

Network B:

Resource access model:

_____

Geographical extent:

_____

Transmission media:

_____

Topology:

_____

Hardware:

_____

_____

_____

_____

_____

_____

Network sketch: